Forgiving, Forgetting, and Moving On

Forgiving, Forgetting, and Moving On

Living a Less-Conflicted Life

Robert E. Hooberman, PhD

JASON ARONSON
Lanham • Boulder • New York • Toronto • Plymouth, UK

Published by Jason Aronson
An imprint of Rowman & Littlefield Publishers, Inc.
A wholly owned subsidiary of The Rowman & Littlefield Publishing Group, Inc.
4501 Forbes Boulevard, Suite 200, Lanham, Maryland 20706
http://www.rowmanlittlefield.com

Estover Road, Plymouth PL6 7PY, United Kingdom

British Library Cataloguing in Publication Information Available

Library of Congress Cataloging-in-Publication Data

Hooberman, Robert E.
Forgiving, forgetting, and moving on : living a less-conflicted life / Robert E. Hooberman.
p. cm.
Includes bibliographical references and index.
ISBN 978-0-7657-0667-6 (cloth : alk. paper) — ISBN 978-0-7657-0669-0 (electronic)
1. Character. 2. Personality. 3. Personality disorders—Treatment. 4. Forgiveness. I. Title.
BF818.H66 2010
158—dc22
2010037653

The paper used in this publication meets the minimum requirements of American National Standard for Information Sciences—Permanence of Paper for Printed Library Materials, ANSI/NISO Z39.48-1992.

Printed in the United States of America

To Nat

Contents

	Preface	ix
Chapter 1	Introduction	1
	Part I: The Bedrock of the Psyche	**7**
Chapter 2	The Nature of the Psyche	9
Chapter 3	Finding the Past in the Present	25
	Part II: Who Am I, and How Did I Get This Way?	**43**
Chapter 4	The Problem-Solving Mind	45
Chapter 5	The Complex Mind	61
Chapter 6	The Partitioned Mind	83
	Part III: Can I Be Different Than I Have Always Been? If So, How?	**93**
Chapter 7	Therapeutic Interventions	95
Chapter 8	Forgiving, Forgetting, and Moving On	121
	References	151
	Index	155
	About the Author	159

Preface

As with anyone who writes in the psychotherapy world, my inspiration comes from my work with patients. From the beginning of my career I have always been fascinated by the workings of the mind. Over the years my enthusiasm for my work has not waned a bit; rather it has intensified as I have gained more experience, expertise and maturity. Writing about my work is not only rewarding in and of itself but also allows me greater access to thoughts not fully articulated. And this is no different from the work of therapy, where we endeavor to bring to awareness that which resides beneath the surface, sometimes just a bit below, and sometimes in places that are very difficult to access. We aim to release inhibited and strangulated affects so that patients also become enlivened and enraptured with their inner worlds.

In my past two books, I have concentrated on character structure as the framework of the psyche. I continue in that vein, but this time turn my attention more specifically to matters of conflict—how it develops, how it can be disabling, and how techniques can be utilized to work through seemingly untenable and unsolvable conflicts into more satisfying solutions.

Most of this book contains new material, but I have gone over some concepts that I touched upon in previous books. I have also strived to make this work accessible to therapists who might not have familiarity in intensive and long-term psychodynamic/psychoanalytic work. It is also my hope that those not in mental health professions but interested and curious on the workings of the psyche, in general and more specifically related to conflict will also find the book rewarding. I further envision that those who have more experience with depth therapy will find my conceptions to be helpful.

My patients have graciously permitted me to describe their therapies. I very much appreciate their willingness to share their stories and struggles and to allow me access into their most vulnerable of places. The gains achieved in our work are clearly mutual.

CHAPTER ONE

Introduction

One might notice that I did not use the term a *nonconflicted* life in my title. In an earlier work (Hooberman, 2007), I wrote, "Conflict is impossible to avoid. The elimination of *some* conflict in life is a reasonable goal, but it may be more helpful to think about how conflicts can become less controlling, less self-destructive, and less paralyzing" (68). Friction between others and between competing ideas and desires can create frustrating and unmanageable hostility, anxiety or other dysphoric feelings that block effective resolutions *or* can impel us to come up with compromises or solutions that can not only calm the parties involved but can spur them on to reach greater heights of satisfaction, and to deeper and more satisfying relationships. So the question is not how to avoid conflict, but how to work it through, productively enhancing creativity while not getting stuck in hostility, guilt and revenge.

I imagine that all of us are at times perplexed by our feelings, thoughts and behaviors. In a split second we find ourselves embroiled in conflicts, saying and doing things that we regret moments later. Or, we find ourselves beset with anxiety and distress over what seem to be small and insignificant events, or over what may seem to others as relatively insignificant transgressions. Or, we question; how do we come to relative peace when we have behaved badly, or how do we come to grips with others' misbehaviors? Forgiving oneself or others may not always be fitting, forgetting often represents denial more than accommodation and yet moving beyond conflict to beneficial solutions is often hard to achieve, and sometimes seems beyond hope. My previous book (Hooberman, 2007) concentrated on integrating various psychodynamic theories in the interpretive process. Although I am using character structure again as my theoretical foundation, this work will concentrate more specifically on paths toward more successful conflict resolution, and will elucidate other areas of psychic functioning not previously addressed.

My wish for this book is that clinicians and those interested in their internal psychological workings can find new perspectives to understand how and why we become overcome with conflict, and develop methods to work through these conflicts in a fashion that respects underlying reasons for conflict but also provides new avenues for thought, feeling and action.

Defining Conflict

Conflict can be considered to be a clash between different people, or between different aspects of a given individual. On first glance it would seem that without undue difficulty we can identify when we are in conflict with another person, although even this seemingly obvious situation can be obscured. For instance, a patient may describe being unhappy and distraught but without any clue as to the origins of his discontent and it is only upon close questioning that it is discovered that the person is dreadfully unhappy in a sterile marriage.

How often do we think that we might want to pursue some activity but become inhibited by some anxiety or sense of foreboding? This is representative of an internal conflict between two aspects of the self. Struggling with competing desires is not necessarily problematic. It is only when these disparate wishes create paralysis or discomfort that we consider them dysfunctional. In the next few chapters, I will be elaborating on aspects within the personality that can operate rather smoothly and enhancing *or* that can become disabling and incapacitating.

Internal and external conflicts are often two sides of the same coin. Internal struggles often become expressed in interpersonal conflicts, such as when another person "pushes our buttons" and we suddenly become enraged. In most cases the buttons being pushed are representative of existing internal conflicts, pushed toward the outside by the stimulus of the aggravating acquaintance or loved one. As we go on we will take a look at this correspondence between inside and outside.

Case Examples

Joyce (whom I wrote about in Hooberman, 2007) was clearly distressed upon entering my consultation room. She tells me that she had backed her car into another the day before and had damaged both. She was furious with herself, and had, as was her custom when blaming herself and in order to relieve tension, beaten herself on her head with her fists. This provided some relief from her anguish. I wondered out loud if there was some other way for her to deal with her distress. "You always say that," she replied. "But when I'm angry or upset, I don't know what to do with the feelings. How do I get rid of them?" Joyce has what I will refer to as a *discharge* problem. When in distress, she doesn't know how to feel better except by *doing* something, and this something is to *rid* her of feelings, often by self-destructive actions.

This technique of affect management was not new to us, and is not unknown to many others. Joyce had demonstrated it many, many times, and although she has made considerable progress in feeling better and in understanding herself more, she still returns to her tried and true self-abuse method of resolving internal conflict. In these times, Joyce would beseech me to tell her "how" to resolve the surging tension she felt when faced with frustration. I have told her that, firstly, I don't have the specific answers that she desires, as I don't have access to an instruction manual on how to deal with conflict and, further, that she was not asking me to help her to resolve her problems in order that she could understand and deal with present and future conflicts more productively, but rather to tell her "how" she could *discharge* or *rid* herself of her feelings (wishing me to be essentially identical to her overly intrusive mother who relentlessly directed and controlled her life). She reluctantly agreed that understanding and gradual dissipation of affect is preferable over her older methods. Why reluctantly? Like everyone else she has developed symptoms (self-abuse) that while awful in one sense, do offer relief and some pleasure in another, and she has trepidation in giving up relief and satisfaction for the possibility of an uncertain outcome via a foray into a different world of thinking and feeling.

Marie, a thirty-five-year-old woman requested an appointment; she indicated that she was depressed and angry. Her primary care physician had attempted to alleviate her despair by prescribing antidepressant medication. Yet Marie felt that she did not only want symptom relief (which wasn't achieved by the medication anyway) but wanted more understanding about the underpinnings of her unhappiness. As we began to talk, she informed me that she was despondent, and enraged with her husband as he had obtained a vasectomy without informing her. She went on to describe how they had four children, ranging in ages from eight to two, but that she very strongly had wanted two more, and couldn't understand her husband's refusal to go along with her plans. Even more galling was that he would make such a major decision as obtaining a vasectomy without consulting her. And, of course, the vasectomy, so long as she stayed married to him, precluded further pregnancies. We spoke more over the next several sessions, allowing her to elaborate on her feelings, and for me to obtain more background information.

At that point, I suggested that I meet with her husband to see what he had to say. She was agreeable to that, and Luke and I met soon thereafter. He informed me that he felt he had few options prior to getting the vasectomy, as his wife was adamant about having more children, and refused to compromise in any way. He had felt completely steamrolled in terms of how many children they were to have as he had only wanted two, and felt that he could compromise to have three, but his wife would have none of it, and was insistent on her plan to have six children. He wanted to stay married, but couldn't conceive how he could do so with their emotions so volatile and negative.

In meeting with Luke he gave me the needed permission to disclose to his wife what he had told me. Marie and I met, and with great bitterness said to me, "I can't understand why he can't get how important—how crucial it was to me to have a large family." I responded, "Perhaps it's equally hard for you to understand that he may have felt equally strong in the opposite direction." She was taken aback, having never really considered this (despite that her husband had made the same point) as she was blinded by her intensity and insistence of her desire (more about his later). This was the turning point in the therapy. It took an outside empathic observer to help to reframe her situation. We continued to ponder this lack of *her* empathy for her husband, and to wonder at her difficulty in listening to her husband's point of view. Luke came in with her for a few sessions, and with my assistance, each spoke about how painful the last several years had been. Luke took some time before he was able to calm down. He was furious and hurt that his wife had disregarded his wishes so completely, and that it had taken a "complete stranger" (me) for her to finally hear what he had been saying all along. During the last two pregnancies he was unexcited and uninvolved, and although physically present at the deliveries, was emotionally absent. He loved his children, but tended to take little responsibility for their care. "She wanted them—it's up to her to take care of them." In fact, this is what she had stated was the sacrifice she would make if they had a large family. But she certainly didn't expect such hostility and indifference, and he was disappointed that he couldn't manage to have a better relationship with his children, that he had surrendered his relationship with them. Now each was resentful and unable to get beyond these past hurts, conflicts and betrayals. As we talked this through, and as they began feeling less angry, they asked me—"How do we move on from here? There is so much hurt and anger. How can we get beyond it, and get our relationship back to where it once was?"

Luke and Marie, in some sense, were asking some of the same questions that Joyce asked. How are uncomfortable feelings worked through in a way that is not destructive, either to the other or to the self? How should one deal with hurts and anger? By forgiving? By forgetting what had transpired? How do relationships recover from conflict? I thought that these were excellent questions and I realized that since everyone faces these dilemmas numerous times throughout life, in relationships of all sorts, and a careful examination of how to work out conflict in healthy ways would be an interesting project for me to pursue; it would be helpful to many, those within the psychotherapy world as well as consumers or potential consumers of this service, or to those interested in understanding more about conflict and pathways toward resolution.

Joyce was also struggling with a common wish—a desire for a clear-cut and defined pathway out of her internal conflicts. In other words, she wished for what I thought were simple answers to complex problems. Many in our world feel similarly, and when these answers are not forthcoming, turn to self-destructive soothing techniques (overeating, drinking to excess, self-punishment, or other acting out behaviors). Those who cannot soothe themselves or interact effectively with others exemplify another question that I would like to address. How can internal and external struggles be laid more to rest by using one's mind to ponder, to wonder—to be curious, and inquisitive, rather than being condemning and punitive? If this positive turn occurs, one can then use that self-generated thoughtfulness for more productive actions.

I am dividing my exposition on conflict into three parts—the first two are on developing an understanding of character structure and its component parts, and the third on therapeutic modes toward conflict resolution and on developing pathways that can enable individuals to move on beyond uncomfortable conflict.

It is my hope that these ideas developed from my years of experience will enable the reader, clinician or otherwise, to help oneself and others to move toward a life less controlled by inner conflict and turmoil, in a way that promotes self-understanding and internal change without promising the impossible and over-idealized notion of easy answers to complex problems, or to living a life without any conflict and tension.

PART ONE

THE BEDROCK OF THE PSYCHE

Character structure is the bedrock of the psyche. My approach in understanding my patients and in fashioning helpful interventions derives from my attention to many aspects of character structure. I see personality as reasonably consistent across varied levels of consciousness. As such, conflicts that are seen in the conscious and preconscious minds will also be found in the unconscious. Attention to character structure affords access at all of these layers.

Those seeking treatment may know that they are depressed or having marital problems, for examples, and may even have a theory as to the origin of the difficulties, but they still struggle to find an explanation that clears the discord. Thus, the first point of business for the therapist and the patient is to work collaboratively, to clarify as much as possible the nature of the conflicts, and then to form a picture of the underlying dynamics. In the two chapters to follow, I will establish how attributes of the psyche develop from internalized representations of significant people in the child's life, and of their perceived relationships with each other, and that seeds of conflict emerge from collisions between disparate and competing aspects of the internal world.

CHAPTER TWO

The Nature of the Psyche

Character Structure

Character structure is the vantage point into the psyche that I have found most useful. Character structure, in the way that I'm using the term, is neither moral judgment about a person—as in is he a good or bad person?—nor diagnoses—as in does he suffer from character pathology? Rather, it describes the totality of our enduring selves. It is the bits and pieces of self and experience that become melded into a complex and reasonably stable personality structure. Some might object to this, though, indicating that many individuals are marked by lability of thought, affect and action, and thereby not stable. But their instability is reliable and somewhat predictable. Thus, although a borderline patient might exhibit a level of instability in terms of affect or in ability to sustain relationships, the instability is a generally consistent quality of the patient (Kernberg, 1967).

How does character structure differ from a person's sense of self, or identity? Generally when we speak of an individual's identity we are referring to the ineffable quality that delimits an individual—that which makes me "me" and you "you." One's sense of identity is not completely conscious as it includes aspects of self that operate automatically and that we may not have cause to think deeply about. Character structure, on the other hand, refers to a more complete rendering of the individual's internal psychic apparatus, encompassing not only a sense of identity, but also more complicated and hidden operating procedures, internal identifications, affects, conflicts, defenses, secrets and other mysteries in all levels of consciousness.

As adults we are a compendium of a complex set of personality dynamics that emerge from multiple influences. The development of character structure is most greatly impacted by the incorporation of family patterns of relating. Fraiberg felicitously referred to this as the "ghosts in the nursery," an intergenerational passing down of characteristic ways of thinking, feeling and behaving (Fraiberg, Adelson and Shapiro, 1987).

Attachment, separation and individuation patterns formed from parent-child relationships persist into adulthood, and manifest themselves interpersonally. One's affective life and nature of affect management are strongly influenced by the interaction of temperament with the quality of parent-child interactions. Emotional "sore spots" that bespeak conflict as well as modes of conflict management are often passed down from generation to generation.

Despite highlighting this intense connection between parent and child, I am not suggesting that children are clones of their parents but only that certain crucial and enduring patterns become established through the parent-child interaction. Yet each child is unique and it is the mix of constitutional variables, family relations, circumstances of life and the distinctiveness of the individual that creates fascinating and complex personality configurations.

Let's look a bit closer at the processes that create the psyche.

From Outside to Inside

In the first chapter, I spoke about the correspondence between internal and external conflict. How does the *external* (the child's experience of her parents' and their relationships) become internalized into the psyche? The young child is an eagle-eyed observer of her parents. Watch children and their parents walk down the street and notice the similar gait; listen to them speak and their language and lexicon are remarkably in tune with each other. Without modeling and identification children would be without navigational skills to move through the world.

Freud famously referred to the identification and internalization process as "when the shadow of the object fell upon the ego" (Freud, 1917, 249). In other words, young children automatically identify with their parents or caregivers: the "objects" referred to by Freud (an "object" is the internalized rendition of a person that has emotional significance for the individual). After identifying with them, children bring these identifications into their internal psychic world. They take into their egos aspects of their parents and of their relationship to each other, and the relationship of each parent to the child, and it is these internalizations that make a significant contribution to the development of a personality structure.

We can refer to the internalized experience of the self as *self-representation*, and internalized experience of others, as *object-representations* (both include conscious and unconscious aspects). Both self and object representations and the perceived relationships between the two are formed from experience and are subjective; in other words not "objectively" true, but idiosyncratic to the person doing the perceiving (Sandler, 1983). These representations form a reasonably stable template from which a child views the self, within relationships and independent of them. They represent expectations of how relationships work, or do not work, and express how the individual characteristically expects to experience the physical, the interpersonal and the emotional worlds. These internal representations are the foundation of character structure.

As I have said, internalizations do not represent "objective" reality. What is perceived depends on the perspective of the perceiver. Consider two groups of parents watching their children playing soccer, and how each side is sure they are correct during a disputed call. This is "subjectivity" and the child is a champion of subjectivity. Children are necessarily egocentric and, especially when young, believe that the universe that they and their parents occupy is the only one that is important, and that the child is the center of that universe. Children often make "attribution errors." For instance, if mother is mad at father, the mother may be irritable when Nancy asks for help, and if this happens often enough the child may internalize a sense that she is bad when she asks for help (she attributes her mother's anger to her "misdeed" of asking for assistance), when in "reality" she was treated poorly because mother was preoccupied with a troublesome marriage, and was unable to address her daughter's needs. When she grows up she may find it difficult to ask others for help since she has internalized this sense of badness when needful. This would be part of her self-representation and her corresponding object-representation would be the expectations that others will be angry with her if she wishes something from them. This is still a very general conception of Nancy and of one particular issue, and one aspect of it. As Nancy grows up this issue will become elaborated in many ways, and will influence her behavior, thoughts and feelings, in very complex and hidden ways. This dynamic is the "tip of the iceberg" and the process of therapy is to explicate both visible and submerged aspects.

Constructions

If we think about the brief soccer example above, we could say that each group of parents is "constructing" their own sense of "reality." They could not reach consensus on what "really" happened. Individuals have their own constructions as to the nature of what they feel are "real." For instance, when Marie rebuffs Luke sexually he feels rejected and misunderstood. When he approaches Marie for sex, she feels put-upon and exploited. Each then responds based upon each one's construction of the "real" meaning of the sexual invitation (Sandler and Sandler, 1987).

Much of how we think of others, the world and ourselves are "constructions." Identifying how each participant views and "constructs" the world is a crucial endeavor during psychotherapy (more about this later). Most people are quite wedded to their sense of reality and part of the process of therapy is to assist individuals to understand the underpinnings of constructions and to free them to look at other perspectives that can be more productive.

Implicit, Explicit, and Atmospheric Memories

Self and object representations accrue meaning from the accumulation of experience. The presence of affect is necessary for these experiences to be memorable. These affectively charged experiences become processed in our memory systems.

These memory systems become activated by current activities that have a resemblance to past incidents. Interpreting the connections between past and present can be greatly beneficial in helping patients cope with present-day emotionally intense situations; in other words, to assist them to understand that they are unwittingly "constructing" a perspective based upon past experiences.

Explicit or episodic memory refers to specific memories—such as when Nancy remembers a ferocious argument between her parents. The terrified child retains that image and believes that it occurred because she was a bad little girl for wanting father to love her more than he did mother. *Implicit* or procedural memory refers to automatic behavior, i.e., when repeated conflict in the family creates an aspect of Nancy's personality that is automatically conflict averse. *Atmospheric* memory relates to the *feel* in a given situation—as when Nancy as an adult becomes terrified when she views others arguing—the smell of disagreement triggers past nonspecific memories of unbearable "tension in the air."

The memory systems I am describing link the present with the past, but do not specifically describe what may be transpiring in a person's mind in a conflictual situation, in any given moment. Discovering and uncovering specific conscious, preconscious and unconscious contents is an essential part of the therapeutic process. A closer look:

Explicit

Maggie (described in Hooberman, 2007) was traumatized in a number of ways growing up. Her brother drowned when she was nine and he was two. Understandably this (explicit memory) was traumatic for the entire family, and emblematic of the pervasive neglect in the household. After the tragedy her parents' already high level of volatility careened out of control, putting her and her siblings at emotional and physical risk. As an adult, Maggie was extremely solicitous of her husband, always very concerned about his heath and well-being. At one point in therapy, she described how she called the dentist to make an appointment for him. I wondered why he couldn't do this for himself. She became quite emotional and tearful and said that she was concerned that he wouldn't if she didn't. I remarked on her strong emotions. She stated that she was very worried about his health, but couldn't really understand why her feelings were so strong. As she discussed this she associated to an *explicit* memory (never told to me before) of watching helplessly while her family members ineffectively tried to revive her brother after finding him in the water. It was a horrifying memory, and it became clear that she identified her husband with her brother, and was afraid that she might, like her parents, just "stand by" and watch as her husband put himself in great danger. However, her over-concern about her husband was also motivated by her defended-against anger toward him for a number of qualities of his that she felt aggrieved by, including his stubborn refusal to take better care of himself.

The last point about Maggie—that is, regarding her anger and her defense against it—is illustrative of many of the specific affects and defensive apparatus that "reside" within an individual's psyche and provide motivational impetus for much of one's behavior.

Implicit

The implicit system describes an individual's way of being, in a sense, her "rules of engagement," templates of expectations, or algorithms to guide one in life. Affects associated with the implicit are not always accessible to direct identification since they are often not verbalized. I described the "implicit" level of personality functioning in my previous book (Hooberman, 2007) and I quote from that work:

> Each of us has a range of such *implicit* phenomena that is unique to us and permeates the way we present ourselves. The implicit represents both our public and private selves. It pervades our essence, our sense of identity, and our sense of being in the world. Although its natural home is in the preconscious, it is

> potentially accessible to consciousness, and it offers a path to the unconscious as well, speaking to family identifications on an intimate and microscopic level. Since it lives, so to speak, in the preconscious, implicit material is potentially available to patient and therapist, although it may not be known until it can be made explicit and so identified. It is apparent more in the "feel" of the patient than in the "content" that he or she produces. (16)

Even more than just by the explicit trauma of the death of her brother, Maggie was subjected to frequent criticism and abuse. She reacted to these over-stimulations by, to the extent possible, removing herself emotionally from affect-laden situations. As an adaptation to the extreme nature of her distressing experiences, her goal in life was to be "cool, calm and collected." This technique was effective in helping her to get through her early life, enabling her to not be derailed by excessive affect. This solution, though, was problematic since her emotional life only had two switches— "on" or "off." She was cool, calm or collected *or* overcome by emotion; modulation was not in her repertoire. Maggie's mode of being, attempting to always be calm and not emotional was automatic, and was as natural to her as riding a bike. It didn't take thought or consideration—it was "just her."

Another aspect of implicit memory can be thought of as "memory in the body." In other words, when actual memory of events is not possible, bodily sensations are representations of early events that were too traumatic to be remembered explicitly (Droga, 1997). In psychotherapy with those of a traumatic background (and this is often a lengthy process), patients can become able to verbalize at least some aspects of previously repressed nonverbalized events alleviating some and sometimes all of the physical symptoms.

Atmospheric

Events that occur in the present may also evoke atmospheric memories. Whenever Maggie felt interpersonal tension, for instance, witnessing two automobile drivers gesturing angrily to each other, she became exceedingly anxious, as it reminded her of the ever-present hostile atmosphere in the family. As another example, Maggie hates the feel—the lights, the parties, trees, etc., of Christmas and never understood why. At a point in the therapy when she was again girding herself against feeling so distressed at Christmas time, she began speaking of the fairly recent death of her sister and how this holiday reminded her of her sister's passing. I wondered if it also reminded her of her brother's death (which occurred in August). Maggie became very sad but still couldn't make the connection. I suggested to her that Christmas is supposed to be a time of joy and hope and that any wishes for his return must have been cruelly disappointing. I also wondered whether the atmosphere of holidays must have been infused with sadness over awareness of the missing child. She responded by being able to speak with great sadness over the more recent death of her sister, and of the hard to remember death of her brother and its terrible aftermath. The "feel" in the family was forever altered, but never spoken about.

Memory and Formulation

How and what a patient remembers is part of the character structure and developing a picture of this is part of the formulation process. When I view how Maggie reacts with fear to what seem to be benign provocations, I can make some preliminary assumptions about the quality of her upbringing. Absolute verification is never possible, but over time, Maggie repeats this behavior time and again, and we link it up with her explicit memories. We develop a memory picture that might not be veridical, but is probably close enough to provide resonance with her experiences and is emotionally relieving when links between past and present are made. Transference reactions (transferring feelings and fantasies from past core relationships onto the therapist) are another source of "memory." Maggie may not have the ability to specifically identify aspects of her relationship with mother, but the manner in which she relates to me is a sort of "memory in action."

When I evaluate a patient and create an assessment of the patient's difficulty—in other words, a description of the problem and possible causes—it is not just the specific events that matter, but also the patterned interactions and the nonverbalized emotion that the child felt that are retained in memory as explicit, implicit and atmospheric memories—conflictual ones and more benevolent ones as well. Although I have presented them separately, they are intertwined and rarely exist independent of each other. Awareness of these memory systems provides for the therapist an effective way of linking past and present. In the next chapter I will delve more deeply into we how strive to help our patients to remember events that have been made inaccessible.

But now I will turn to elaborate the connection between past relationship patterns and present-day functioning.

Luke and Marie

I will first demonstrate with Luke how past parent-child relationships impact upon character, particularly on his self and object representations. Following that I will do the same with Marie and see how their identifications and internalizations have affected their present-day relationship. I will also describe with each how their different experiences have impacted their character structure, including implicit, explicit and atmospheric memory systems.

Luke's History

Luke was the first in his immediate family to go to college let alone to obtain a graduate degree. He was raised in a small midwestern city where both parents worked in what could be considered to be lower-middle-class occupations. His father had played semipro football in his youth and was obsessed in Luke's football career, having been frustrated in his own. In undergraduate school, Luke was a lackluster student, believing that his future lay in football. A pivotal moment occurred in his junior year when he took a class in biomedical engineering. The professor was kind and smart, and recognized Luke's intellectual potential. Being mentored by a positive and affirming father figure, Luke gradually transitioned his intensity from football to schoolwork. His relatively poor grades initially made entrance into graduate school difficult but he persevered and was eventually admitted to a fine university to study engineering. He did well there and obtained an excellent postgraduate position in a research facility run by a world-class scientist. Even though most would consider these accomplishments as an indication of his capability, Luke still doubted himself in part due to the fact that although he believed he had come to terms with his football history, his father had not, convinced that Luke could have "made it" to professional football had he persevered. Luke's ambivalence toward his father (wanting to please yet resenting the pressure) created internal ambivalence toward his own accomplishments.

Luke is the oldest of two, and clearly both more favored and more successful than his younger brother. In our sessions Luke initially expressed very strong positive and admiring feelings toward his father. He felt his father was a man of integrity. Perhaps he wasn't the warmest of fathers but made up for it in his interest in his son and his general positive attitude. Mother was described as being quite cold, sour and distant, neither warm nor affectionate. She seemed rather judgmental and negative. The parental relationship was conflictual and not especially loving, and apparently close to divorce at times. Luke remembered intense arguments and periods of icy relations between his parents. In more recent times the parents seem to have reached some sort of semipeaceful coexistence.

Let's now see how his background has impacted his character structure and consequently his patterns of affect and conflict management. As I have said, despite his success, Luke retained a sense of being second best, and often shied away from confrontation. When at odds with those senior and superior to him, he felt anxious and racked with guilt should he not think of others' interests ahead of his own. He remembered his father telling him to put his own ambitions behind those of the team. His father also seemed to have not felt comfortable in asserting himself, often deferring to others. Those who were aggressively self-aggrandizing also caused Luke discomfort resulting first in uncomfortable withdrawal and second in self-blame for not being more assertive.

Although his father was proud and supportive, he also recalled times when his father would "joke" about his shortcomings or past misdeeds. These caused intense feelings of shame and anger but he would no more tell his father this than fly to the moon. Direct confrontation between children and parents was not exactly forbidden in his family, but "just wasn't done" and might invite further derision. Luke never really felt close to his mother and affection between them was infrequent and awkward. Even with his wife he felt uncomfortable expressing feelings of care and tenderness although it was apparent to me that he loved her a great deal.

We knew that he had difficulty with anger from these various episodes and from his earlier conflict with his wife over the number of children to have, but he also provided more information later on in the therapy. He told me that when upset with his wife, or with his parents, he would "freeze them out," and he said this with great anger and intensity. These "freeze outs" occurred when his parents did not call as frequently as he thought they should, or when his wife was not interested in sex, but he did not realize his anger was a defense against feeling hurt and weak until I suggested this to him.

Luke was raised in an atmosphere of conflict and distrust. He felt loved by his father, yet received more ambivalent feelings from mother. He felt her to be lost and empty. His father was more present and involved but this too could be problematic. His father had placed great stock in Luke's athletic abilities, wanting to gain his own self-esteem from his son's athletic successes. Having a father desiring to soothe his disappointments through his son can be hazardous, in at least three ways. First of all, Luke is not trying to achieve athletic success solely for himself—his father has a lot riding on it, placing too much pressure on the son. Secondly, in these kinds of situations, the father's competitiveness can lurk unseen, and push him toward behavior that actually undermines his son. We can see this by his not infrequent disparaging remarks. Lastly, the natural competitiveness and aggression between father and son becomes too strongly activated, resulting in Luke internalizing a difficult conflict between loving and hating feelings.

Luke in the Present

So let's see how all of this has affected Luke. Luke internalized aspects of his parents' attributes, of their relationship, and of their relationship to him. Luke does not feel unsatisfied with his football career. However, the feeling of having disappointed his father creates the sense that he is not successful in his current career. Like his father, Luke is highly competitive, but because of concerns about being more successful than father, Luke tends to underplay his abilities, and views those who are senior or superior with trepidation, as they are stand-ins for his father toward whom his ambivalence is unsettling.

Aversion toward "superiors" is especially present with those whom he finds to be disparaging. His solution is to back down, and then to feel inadequate and inferior. If he would challenge these more aggressive father symbols, he would feel guilty, as he is not really challenging these contemporary figures, but his father in effigy, and he is afraid that his degree of hostility would be unmanageable. His father had seemingly blocked his own anger, not providing Luke with a model, and making Luke's typical anger toward his father seem dangerous and forbidden.

Like his father, Luke is hard working and responsible, and certainly seems warm and caring to me. Yet, like his mother he can become cold and distant, as when he "freezes" others out. His relationship with his wife is certainly much better than that of his parents, but at times he becomes cold and uncaring. He can also feel awkward with affection (similar to that of his parents). He is reluctant to commit to therapy, fearing that it is an indication of weakness and dependency. These feelings spill over into his marriage, too, preventing a closer relationship with Marie. And in some ways Luke and Marie run very separate lives, again not that different from either of their parents' relationships.

In this summary, I have described how Luke has internalized aspects of his childhood self (self-representation), his parents (object representations) and of their relationship. These internalizations color how he views the world, how he deals with affects, and in relation to our present purpose, to conflict management, notably with his wife, but in other areas of his life as well.

What about his memory systems? I have already mentioned the *atmospheric*—that of conflict and distrust. Thus, despite going into his marriage consciously loving and trusting his wife, it didn't take long for conflict and distrust in the present to raise their ugly heads. It didn't help that he felt betrayed by her when they were deciding on the size of their family. *Implicitly*, Luke is afraid of being revealed as some kind of fraud, not as capable as he is making himself out to be. This is a consequence of the unacknowledged and unprocessed disparagement he suffered at the hands of his father. In addition, with a depressed mother he never felt that he earned her love, could never make her happy, like all boys wish. This added to an implicit sense of himself as being not quite capable. Explicitly, Luke recalls a "game" with father and his uncles where the older men took turns hitting Luke and his cousins on the arms, with the stated object for the boys was to neither cry nor whine. Those that did either were labeled as weak and sissy-like.

Luke's positive sense of himself was negatively impacted from *explicit* memories of his relationship with his parents and family, from more *implicit* memories or beliefs of being a disappointment to his parents, and from the memory of the *atmosphere* of conflict and distrust.

Marie's History

Now Marie. Marie is also the oldest, but of four. She gets along well with her siblings but silently objects that she is always put in the position of buying gifts for their parents or arranging reunions. She doesn't remember any specific conflicts with her brothers or sister but finds the sister somewhat bossy and critical.

When not caring for her children, she works as a lawyer in a local legal aid society. She took this position because of social conscience beliefs and since it offered her the opportunity to work part-time. One of her other brothers is a lawyer as well, but he works in a high-powered firm and makes scads of money. The other brother works in sales, and her sister is a physician.

Marie was an exceptional student and went to one of the best schools in the country, for both undergrad and law school. Part of her intense desire to do so well was due to the fact that she quaked at the idea of ever being perceived negatively. If this happened or if she imagined that it had happened, she would become ashamed and furious. She drove herself very hard and had trouble accepting her imperfections. Marie had had some unfortunate early adolescent and college dating experiences, both of which involved unwanted sexual contact; neither of which she ever disclosed to either parents or husband. The college experience was difficult but the earlier episode made her feel confused, ashamed and betrayed by a teenage boy that she had thought was her friend.

In describing her parents it was apparent that her feelings about them were a source of discomfort. The parents never really got along very well, and Marie felt undone by their frequent squabbles. Her father was perfectionistic and bombastic. Although a teacher with regular and reasonable hours of work, he was often gone in the evening and there was some suspicion that he was having affairs. Like Luke, Marie was an athlete, but her sport was soccer. She was an excellent midfielder but remembered episodes where she felt intensely nervous before and during games and she linked these feelings to her concern over being berated by her father for what he perceived as poor play. The father was outwardly contemptuous of those that he viewed as less smart or successful than he was. And this particularly included his wife, who he belittled by calling "stupid." Although he was hard on others, he often seemed to have endless excuses for his own misbehavior (staying out, never following through on tasks or promises, being verbally abusive). Father ruled the roost and controlled and dominated the children and their mother. He bragged about his children's accomplishments in a self-aggrandizing fashion that greatly embarrassed Marie, and made her feel that her accomplishments were more for father than for herself.

Marie's mother was quite self-effacing, lacked self-respect and was depressed. She worked as a paraprofessional at the same school where her husband worked and to her shame never made much money. The mother rarely stood up to her husband and constantly felt aggrieved. Her parents fought about many things, money being one of them. Father was very tight and begrudged anything that mother wished to purchase. Being paid less, she was at a disadvantage. Despite or perhaps because of being the butt of withering criticism (from both husband and *her* mother), she was notably hypercritical of her children and of the manner in which they raised their children.

Marie's mother was embittered by the fact that her marriage was forced by an unwanted pregnancy (of Marie), and her disclosure of this to Marie did not do much to enhance Marie's sense of being loved and valued. And she also expressed to Marie that this was a fate that she was determined that Marie should not endure, not conveying to Marie that she was trusted to make good choices on her own.

Marie in the Present

As described in the first chapter regarding her desire for six children, Marie could be quite insistent and hard headed. When we discussed this she indicated that she had always felt that one should present one's case as forcefully as possible, and the "stronger" case should win. When questioned about this she realized that this technique might be efficacious in legal conflicts but perhaps not in marriages. But she really was lost in figuring out how to solve problems in her marriage in a way that was as fair as possible to both parties.

Anger puzzles and unsettles her, and when in conflicts at work tends to back down, and then in a fashion similar to that of Luke, turn the aggression inward. Because she has trouble distinguishing between hostility and anger (more about this in later chapters), Marie becomes paralyzed with confusion and guilt in conflictual situations.

When she first began psychotherapy she described some events with her children where she felt that she had lost control of her anger on a few occasions and had punished the children too severely. Fortunately, this did not happen too frequently and it didn't take long in treatment for her to be able to tolerate frustrations in a more evenhanded manner. Her difficulty in appreciating her husband's point of view in regards to the pregnancies suggested to me that she had not really been empathized with in growing up and subsequently had trouble being that way with herself and with others. It seemed to me that my empathic responses to her modeled what she needed to do with her children.

Let's now look at her identifications and internalizations. Like both parents, Marie can be hypercritical. Because her parents were so angry, she lacks the ability to process angry feelings comfortably. Instead, like both mother and father she becomes hostile, believing that, in a sense, that "might makes right," and exhibited this conception with her husband over the size of their family. She can be unyieldingly harsh with her own misdeeds, perceived or real, and this harshness has been conveyed to her husband and children at times.

She can be warm and caring but has trouble expressing it to her husband and also feels awkward with affection. Marie's mother would (inappropriately) complain of her father's sexual needs, and this has added to Marie's already formed perception of her father as being exploitative, and she sometimes views Luke's sexual interest similarly. Men seem a bit foreign to her, and she has indicated that she doesn't really trust them (clearly this will have implications for the transference relationship).

She describes a crushing feeling of anxiety in her chest when events feel emotionally challenging. Despite being quite accomplished, she fears never being good enough, a feeling directly transmitted to her from her parents. Because her father was aggravatingly self-aggrandizing, she is reluctant to tell others of her accomplishment, fearful that they will find any such disclosure as obnoxious. With the unconscious collusion of her husband, she has re-created some aspects of the parental relationship. Each live very separate lives with somewhat sporadic attempts at closeness.

What about her memory systems? *Atmospherically*, she feels herself to be in a relationship that *feels* threatening, reminiscent of the atmosphere that was ever present in her household. Even if she and her husband are getting along reasonably well, she still expects the feeling tone to deteriorate at a moment's notice. *Implicitly*, she feels, not unlike Luke, to be less capable than she really is. She also fears being exposed as some sort of fraud, even though she is actually quite competent. *Explicitly* she remembers hurtful comments from her father, and her mother's recounting of Marie's birth as being unwanted has been extremely painful to her and has led to intense feeling of being unwanted and unvalued.

Their Relationship

The reader can easily see the similarities between Luke and Marie. Each has been raised in similar atmospheres of unmanaged anger, conflict and distress. Each had unfulfilled fathers who projected their own aspirations onto their children, while undermining them all the while. Each had mothers who were depressed and negative. Neither had been given the tools to solve conflicts effectively. Each struggled with internal conflicts—struggling to find self-worth, to deal with uncomfortable feelings of anger, of feeling more comfortable in their sexual selves, and with external conflicts—managing anger with others, not allowing others to make them feel bad about themselves. It is not that surprising Luke and Marie have quite remarkable similarities since many couples are more alike than not. Self-love causes us to search out those who have similar dynamics. It is hard to be involved with someone who we cannot sympathize with, and we tend to seek out others who have resonance with ourselves.

Marie's desire for more children despite already having her hands full is an attempt to find an "antidote" for her feelings of being unloved—the more children, the more opportunity to be loved. It also serves to isolate her from her husband, relegating him to a less desired position, just as she felt her station in her family to be.

We can also see how their partners triggered their internal conflicts. Both suffered from feelings of inadequacy, and this and their inability to express their love and affection reinforced the existing gap in their self-esteem. Unmodulated aggression was also problematic and stimulating angry exchanges were not felt to be discussable or resolvable. Each used their own characteristic ways of dealing with hurt and anger on the other.

It is clear that the three of us have our work cut out for us, and having this preliminary understanding of their dynamics and how they intersect and interact will provide us with a framework from which we can pursue deeper understanding and resolution of conflict.

Concluding Thoughts

In this chapter I have concentrated on delineating some of the ways in which character structures develop. In the next chapter I will continue in a similar direction but will hone in on the nature of both fantasies and levels of consciousness and their effect on what does or does not become conflictual. These descriptions will lead toward an elaboration on how conflict emerges from the various forces at play within the individual's psyche.

CHAPTER THREE

Finding the Past in the Present

In the previous chapter I delineated aspects of character structure using Luke and Marie's dynamics as case examples. Continuing from that developmental schema, I will now concentrate on other aspects of the psyche—levels of consciousness, central fantasies and anxieties, and relate these facets to conflict formation.

Conflict often emerges from past experiences that are subjected to defenses that operate to keep painful memories and feelings beyond conscious awareness. An effective therapy assists patients in being able to recapture events that have been relegated to the dustbins of unremembered history, and I will elaborate on this process in this chapter. As before, my supposition is that greater understanding of the factors that create symptomology leads toward greater understanding of conflict and its origin and this in turn provides a pathway towards more effective resolution.

Although this section of the book concentrates mainly on assessment, it must be recognized that assessment and interpretation are often intertwined. The understanding of patient dynamics continues throughout therapy from beginning to end. To this end, I will move a bit into the world of interpretation as this will help to illuminate complex issues on defense, fantasy development and levels of consciousness.

Upstairs-Downstairs

Nonconscious phenomena are often hard to apprehend, since they are, well, nonconscious. The reader will notice that I am referring to *nonconscious* phenomena as opposed to *unconscious* phenomena. *Unconscious* phenomena are usually referred to as thoughts and feelings that the psyche deems dangerous, frightening or forbidden and attempts to keep from becoming conscious by the use of defense mechanisms. The nonconscious system contains defended-against (unconscious) material but also includes many other aspects of mental functioning that are not repressed but still not conscious such as implicit memories, or the automatic operation of defense mechanisms.

To some patients I have suggested that they can think of their conscious minds being "upstairs" and their nonconscious minds being "downstairs." This analogy to illustrate levels of consciousness has been accepted well.

As we really cannot directly view the world of the unconscious ("downstairs"), we need to find other points of entry. Fortunately there are several pathways into that mysterious world. In the following I describe how we can use patients' behavior patterns, thoughts, associations, fantasies and affects to give us a glimpse into their more hidden selves, and to identify conflictual material that is denied access into consciousness because of internal discomfort. Defenses both obscure and illuminate, as will be seen shortly. I will also discuss defensive operations more fully later in the book.

First, different levels of consciousness may operate in parallel; the conscious expressions giving voice to similar unconscious wishes or conflicts. Second, we can look for derivatives that give us clues toward defended-against material. A derivative is a conscious affect, feeling or thought that 'derives' from a hidden affect, feeling or thought, and is allowed consciousness since it does not feel as dangerous, frightening or forbidden. It is the end product of unconscious material that is pushed toward consciousness in disguised or altered form.

Third, we can focus very closely on the patient's flow of associations (free or unfree) and notice sequence of thoughts and/or disruptions in the continuity of thoughts that give indication of conflictual material. Fourth, we can attend to our own affective experiences in our encounter with the patient for "unconscious communication" of underlying material. There are many ways in which people communicate nonverbally. It is uncanny what is transmitted without conscious awareness or intent. Fifth, we can attend to the fashion in which the patient relates to the therapist. The verbal and nonverbal quality of interaction with the therapist (transference-countertransference) is a testament to the nature of early relationships, with both conscious and nonconscious elements. And lastly, at even more of a remove from consciousness, an interpretation may be offered based upon associations that, on the surface, seem to have little to do with significant conflicts, but on closer look offer a path toward understanding hidden material. This type of interpretation is based upon a combination of therapist intuition, his own associations, intimate understanding of the patient's dynamics and identification of the patient's implicit level of functioning. In all of these venues, the therapist's interpretations serve as the "stairs" or the links between the two "floors" of consciousness.

Here are examples; first using the parallel concept. Freud (1900) referred to dreams as the "royal road to the unconscious," indicating that dream analysis plays an important part in understanding one's hidden conflicts. My patient Rachel, age fifty, has recently broken up with a boyfriend and reports a dream: "I see pregnant women, looking beautiful. My cousins are there." I ask for her thoughts. She associates to her father going to Florida; she's not going. She's mad at him because he made his plans and expected her to come regardless of her schedule. Her cousins live in Florida and she likes them well enough yet doesn't really believe her feelings are reciprocated. What about pregnant women? She tells me that the day prior she saw the movie *Juno*, a story about a pregnant teenage girl. Rachel describes the character in very positive terms and with admiration points to the young woman's ability to be direct and straightforward. Juno's father is very supportive and loving. The back story: Rachel has just broken up with a man who couldn't/wouldn't commit, and this wasn't the first man in her life with this unfortunate quality. This is reminiscent of attributes of her father and cousins who are not particularly emotionally present or supportive (the mother's story will be told later in this chapter). She says she is hurt by their disinterest and by her ex-boyfriend's lukewarm attraction but in the telling I don't really discern any strong affects.

In the movie she enviously sees a loving father who encourages Juno to find someone who "loves her for just the way she is" and Juno indeed finds just such a person. In this recounting, Rachel becomes tearful. I ask for her to elaborate on her feelings. She tells me that she wishes that she had a father like Juno's, as she never felt that she had anyone who expressed unconditional love. Rather she felt love was sparse and halfhearted. She tells me all of this with great emotion, which I can also feel. I emphasize (interpret) that even though she intellectually knew that her family was not very warm and comforting, the dream and her associations to the movie enabled her to *feel* what had been previously defended. Her admiration for Juno is also an expression of a more affectively vibrant wish to be like Juno, more direct and straightforward. This material isn't really new, but the dream and her associations to it allowed her to be more in touch with previously submerged affect (downstairs) and gives more meaning to the already conscious and parallel (upstairs) knowledge of the 'reality' of her family constellation.

Now as to a derivative: Maggie describes going on a trip with an acquaintance. When told of this upcoming trip I wondered whether the vacation was going to work out well since there were already indications that Gloria was a rather difficult person. Maggie shrugged off any concern. Unfortunately, during their time together, for reasons unknown to Maggie, Gloria viciously attacked her, calling her selfish and difficult to get along with. Upon her return both Maggie and I were perplexed since neither of us recognized these descriptions as being in her nature. Nevertheless I asked Maggie how she felt when attacked like this. She said that she just figured that Gloria was "having a bad day." "You weren't angry?" I queried. She thought about it a bit and said she didn't think so. I let that statement stand, and suddenly she became quite mad. "I can't believe she said that to me. She's the one that is selfish and difficult to get along with." She elaborated and gave me several examples of Gloria's bad behavior. I then wondered why she had trouble feeling what might seem obvious—that is, understandably angry when attacked. Maggie went on to describe how she felt anger to be dangerous. She was afraid that she might be like her parents and lose control and act out inappropriately. I agreed with her explanation and also suggested that perhaps Gloria's actions were very similar to that of her parents—both parties externalized their shortcomings, and her parents unpredictably blasted her for minor or nonexistent wrongs. By denying the present-day anger and hurt from Gloria's behavior, Maggie was protecting herself from past terribly hurtful feelings. With relief Maggie agreed with my interpretations. We can see that her blasé attitude (upstairs), characteristic of her character style, was a *derivative* of defended-against anger and hurt (downstairs). My interpretation enabled her to realize the nature of her real feelings and she soon thereafter begged off on further contact with Gloria. In doing this she was actually protecting herself from further hurt by recognizing that her defensive denial designed to protect paradoxically kept her involved in a hurtful relationship.

Let's take a look at "free association" or the lack thereof. Free association, the suggestion that patients say whatever comes to mind without censure or desire, may sound easy but is really anything but. Dangerous or forbidden feelings and thoughts often do not reach awareness (downstairs), and even when they do may not be disclosed to the therapist because of conscious shame, guilt or discomfort (upstairs). Both circumstances disrupt communication flow.

Maggie would often fall silent in sessions. Most often she stopped speaking when the topic was threatening or when she was already feeling emotionally overwrought. As can be seen from the situations that I have already described, Maggie had intense conflicts over angry feelings. In speaking about her feelings about another conflictual relationship, it was obvious to me that she was struggling. After talking about them for a while, she fell silent for quite a while. I asked for her thoughts and she described walking the dog the night before and seeing an accumulation of dog feces on the snow banks along the road. She felt disgusted. I wonder out loud if she felt that her angry feelings were disgusting. She agrees and says that she never really thought of that (downstairs) before. From this we now proceed to an examination of why she finds such feelings disgusting and the relevance to her feelings about herself and relationships with others. Due to her traumatic and abusive background it is not surprising that angry feelings trouble her. Her parents were too angry with her too often, frightening her and creating an intensely critical sense of self. As her parents were unable to effectively modulate their feelings, she had no model of effective use of anger, and she has been afraid of discharging her anger irresponsibly, irrationally and out of control. Her attempt to expel (akin to feces) and deny these feelings is also characteristic of her family's mode of affect management. I ask her why she had the thoughts about the feces, but she was reluctant to tell me. She replies, "I'm not sure, but if they are associated with anger, I wouldn't want to tell you. I always feel that angry feelings are unsightly." We can see that her inhibition and defenses are strong; having these feelings seem disgusting and are associated with feces (downstairs), telling me about them feels unsightly (upstairs). We can see the parallel concept here as well. By discussing these feelings, and by elaborating on their sense of danger and of being forbidden and not only "unsightly" but disgustingly associated with feces, she can gain a greater sense of understanding about her conflicts about angry feelings, a sense of being more in control of her emotions and a diminished sense of self-criticism, especially since I am nonjudgmental about any of this.

In terms of listening for sequences, one can listen very carefully to how a patient moves from one theme to another, and identify the pattern as an indicator of an issue of which the patient may not be aware. Marie told me that she took her kids to see a movie, *Madagascar 2*, and in the midst of it felt anxious (upstairs). She was bewildered and upset. She moved on to the next topic. Her mother was visiting. She appreciated the help her mother provided, and the kids enjoy her. She was glad to see her but glad for her to go. After her mother left she and her husband got into a fight. "The subject?" I asked. At first she couldn't remember but now she recalls that she felt irritable with him when he didn't pick up his clothes. At this point I am wondering more about her mother's visit. "Anything of note about the visit?" I ask. "Mmm. Yeah, I can't believe that I forgot this" (downstairs). She goes on to describe how her mother yelled at one of Marie's children for not dressing sufficiently for the cold weather. Marie told her mother that she felt it was okay for the child to dress like that as he was only going to be outside briefly and that cold weather would not cause colds. Her mother emphatically said to Marie, "You're wrong! You're wrong!" Marie felt both angry and chagrined. She then spoke of other instances when her mother was uncharitable, to say the least. Considerable intense emotion was expressed in the recounting of these instances. She then went back to wondering about her reaction at the viewing of the movie. "Tell me about the movie," I asked. Marie told me that the movie was about Alex the Lion who was transported from the Central Park Zoo to the plains of Africa. Alex tried to be "one of the guys" in Africa but was made fun of because of being different. Tears began to flow as Marie was in touch with her constant sense of inadequacy and inhibition in expressing herself for not only the fear of shame-inducing criticism but also for associated intense affects (downstairs). This emotional freeing helped her to talk about another difficult issue with her husband (about her feeling that he disrespected her, in general and specifically with his refusal to pick up after himself) that she had also put out of her mind (in order to not feel his criticism and shame), until the moment in which she became aware of her inhibition and the reasons for it. We can see that this very active and helpful session became so once I focused on her sequence of associations (upstairs) and by what felt to me as a minimizing of the effect (downstairs) of her mother's visit, as well as by pursuing questioning on the theme of the movie.

Unconscious communication: An uncanny experience in psychotherapy is when either participant seems to "read" the others' mind. In truth it is not so much as mind reading as that individuals in relationships derive expectations based on past experiences, and these expectations cause them to unconsciously key in with others' thoughts. Further there is some evidence from neurophysiology about "mirror neurons," which might provide a biologically based understanding of unconscious communications. (Dapretto, 2006). How do we see this in therapy? Sometimes I might have a thought or image that was mysteriously triggered by the patient's verbalizations. Rachel, in the beginning of therapy was describing her mother to me. Her mother died when Rachel was fifteen, and she had not felt much of anything about it then, and now. She knew from a "theoretical" position that she probably suffered from "incomplete mourning" but she did not feel emotionally connected with any sense of loss (upstairs). While listening to Rachel describe her mother I couldn't capture a sense of her as being a real person; instead I found myself thinking about the movie *The Hours*. I thought about the scene where a little boy is anguished, banging on the window as his mother drives away, unaccountably afraid that his mother might not return. We learn soon after that the mother is seriously contemplating suicide.

I informed Rachel of my thoughts and she found them interesting but did not have further thoughts or feelings. Nevertheless, I felt that she was unconsciously (downstairs) conveying to me, in the only way available to her, information as to the nature of her mother and of their relationship, i.e., that she most likely felt some sense of deep despair in relation to her mother, similar to the little boy in the movie. At that time, I didn't make much of the suicidal material in the movie, although I asked Rachel if her mother ever threatened to take her own life but Rachel said no. But a couple of years later, in rummaging in her mother's belongings, she came upon a note that sounded very much like a suicidal one, and it was dated many years before she was diagnosed with her cancer. Unconsciously I keyed into those "unthought knowns" (Bollas, 1987) of Rachel's defended-against despair by associating to material in the movie that, in my mind, was similar to her heretofore unverbalized and unformulated (Stern, 1983) experiences. My conjecture at the time of my internal meandering about *The Hours* which was later confirmed by our further work, was that Rachel avoided intimate relationships for fear of experiencing the defended-against bereft feelings occasioned by both the nature of her relationship with mother (distant and uninvolved) and by the mother's death (and related to her father's less than enthusiastic feelings toward her).

In psychotherapy we often look to the relationship between patient and therapist as an indicator of past relationship patterns. As I mentioned in the previous chapter, identifications are powerful sources of character structure and we tend to relate to others based on our internalization of early object relationships. The transference of old relationship patterns from past to present is not only a potent source of information about the patient's internal world but is an effective avenue toward cure, as can be seen from this next example. James was a bright and engaging young man. He was shorter than he wished, and as he put it "scrawny" and these attributes had always been a source of discomfort and shame. From his description his mother appeared to be occasionally degrading while his father seemed well-meaning but not particularly emotionally sensitive or available. Although his father did not have a height advantage, he was a powerfully built man who worked in construction. James, on the other hand, worked successfully as a financial analyst but never felt quite as strong or capable as he wished, often referencing his slight build. His relationship with his parents was cordial, but he never really felt he got their attention and, to some degree, their respect.

During the therapy I felt that I had a pretty good understanding of his dynamics. I would listen to his associations and make an interpretation that I felt was on the mark, but I would find that he would often nod his head in response but didn't seem to take my thoughts in. Eventually realizing that I felt hurt by his disinterest in my thoughts, I realized that he was being dismissive of me, just as he had felt his parents had been towards him. Furthermore I understood that he needed to deny my "potency" in order not to compare my capabilities with his own, and end up feeling that he came up "short." In response to these thoughts, I said to him that I recently realized that although he was nodding his head in agreement to my thoughts, he didn't really seem to take my interpretations seriously and that felt a bit hurtful. I also told him that from that behavior I could understand how he felt growing up since I felt dismissed just as he had. He was startled by this and indicated that he understood what I meant but didn't really understand why he would behave like this (upstairs). I suggested to him that he could feel better about himself by denying my capabilities (downstairs). From that he was able to speak more emotionally about himself, how hurt he had been by his parents, and how painful all of this had been. And he could see what I meant about being "dissed" and could understand his need to figuratively put me down.

As a consequence of this discussion, he could see the connection between his past conflicts and his feelings about and behavior toward me. This transference-countertransference (I identified his feelings by paying attention to my own, and disclosing them to him in a nonhurtful fashion) work helped to increase his self-esteem as he could reestablish his sense of self in relation to more realistic standards and not in comparison with his childhood view of his father, or because of the hurtful behavior of his mother.

Here is an example of more obscure material. Maggie and I have long suspected that her father sexually abused her. Dreams, associations and the fact that other family members recollect abuse, at his hands, was not absolute proof but pretty confirmatory. Still Maggie was not able to produce specific memories. In the midst of a difficult period during which Maggie was struggling to not feel overwhelmed by the possibility of remembering, she reported the following. Being in the medical field she was privy to talks given at the local university. She had noticed one on esophageal cancer. She told herself she wanted to go since she had reflux, and was concerned over developing the dreadful disease. She described being at home on the day of the presentation. As the time of the talk approached, she became quite upset because she feared that she might miss the talk yet strangely couldn't bring herself to go. She told me that when she looked at the clock time seemed to pass at an agonizingly slow pace, yet couldn't bring herself to leave. She became inexplicably relieved when it was too late to go. She was upset and perplexed. We discussed the situation and I wondered why she felt it so important to attend the talk. "Well I have reflux." I responded, "Sure but . . ." She said, of course, "I don't really need to know this."

We pondered this apparent paradox of wanting and not wanting to go to the presentation. After a while, I wondered about the connection with the esophagus. "Ah," she said with emotion, "since it has to do with swallowing, it might be related to my concerns about performing oral sex on my father," she said. She had had dreams about this and her relative had reported that Maggie's father had forced her to perform oral sex. After considerable discussion and putting together this material with what I knew about how her mind works, I came to a conclusion that seemed to explain the mysterious behavior. I suggested to her that she was unconsciously afraid that the presenter would say one of two things, either that oral sex did or that it did not cause esophageal cancer, and that if she either felt relieved *or* anxious from this information it would confirm to her that she had performed oral sex on her father. On one hand, she wanted to go because she unconsciously desired to find out what had happened to her as a child, yet also wanted reassurance that nothing had happened. But by not going she avoided having any telling reaction, which might have then created frightening and overwhelming feelings. Interpreting this released a rush of tears, and she felt better although still frightened. Although she and I have considerable work to do, I am using this example to show how the "downstairs" (anxiety about remembering, and childhood fantasies about the danger and forbidden aspect of what she had unwillingly participated in—that it would cause disease or death) was interpreted by the "upstairs" of her urgency to both go and to not go to the conference.

Linking present behavior, thoughts and feelings with aspects of varying levels of consciousness, defended against or otherwise, helps to enable the patient to free herself from conflictual forces that interfere with autonomy. Now let's take a closer look at memory and how patients strive to forget events that are painful.

Remembering and Forgetting

A question that I raise in this work regards the advisability of "forgetting" as a road toward conflict resolution. As I will describe below (and in the final chapter), every symptom is a representation of a memory, and the recapture of forgotten memories can free one from the tyranny of repression that, in turn, leads toward a greater ability to understand and confront conflict.

We can't discuss forgetting without referencing its companion of remembering. We can't forget if we have not first registered events in our memory systems. The process of remembering occurs once we perceive an event as significant. Our attention is grabbed by events, feelings or thoughts that are emotionally meaningful, and only when some emotional attachment is established does an activity become memorable. We encode not only explicit events, but also procedures (implicit memories encoded at the preconscious levels), feeling states (atmospheric memories), fantasies (conscious and unconscious)—any activity that the person encounters that is meaningful can become remembered. In this consideration of forgetting aspects of conflict, we are discussing forgetting that occurs in all areas of consciousness.

Nonconscious Forgetting

The defensive apparatus is designed to protect the psyche from becoming aware (remembering) of some painful or forbidden affects or thoughts. Gaining access to the memories in a way that is palatable is one aspect of the work of therapy. The therapist looks to find the past in the present through a number of therapeutic activities. Free associations, dreams, fantasies, transference and countertransference reactions, "feelings in the air," defensive maneuvers, derivatives, unconscious communications, sequence of thoughts, narrative flow—and lack thereof—are enlisted to find the past and then to loosen its hold on the present.

Events that are encoded in seemingly inaccessible memory systems don't cease to exist; rather they are "placed" somewhere in the psyche. In the case of explicit events, these memories reside in the patient's "hard drive," or long term memory. If substantial conflict exists, memories tend to become unconscious. Implicit, automatic or procedural memory find their home in the more accessible conscious and preconscious operating systems of the psyche. As identifying implicit memories is more a matter of making the patient aware of aspects never before thought about as opposed to uncovering repressed memories, we are not focused on "uncovering" something forgotten but on bringing to awareness patterns of relating.

Patients come to therapy with symptoms, and these symptoms represent memories transformed. So even if the patient does not remember the feelings, or dynamics or conflicts that might have led toward the symptom, the patient and therapist can use the symptom as a path toward finding the original stimulating events. For instance, Maggie avoided feelings at almost any cost, and when her defenses failed found herself disgustingly dirty and messy. When distressed she tidied up the house, or occupied her mind with gardening tasks, all designed to put order into what felt like a frighteningly disordered mind. But her maneuvers failed, she was left with overwhelming anxiety. Of course we knew that she had a traumatic history—one brother drowning, another brother being hit by a car when he was a child, a mother who seemed to hate her, a father with inappropriate sexual feelings toward her—all in all too, too much. The anxiety in the present was triggered when situations were too reminiscent of activities that wished to be forgotten.

Maggie put high prominence on remaining cool, calm and collected. With good reason since untoward events would derail her sense of stability. She believed that replacing overt anxiety with denial and disavowal was a good bargain; only to later find that the dysphoria would come forth unbidden and with no warning. The defensive measures she used, although better than despair, were still inadequate to the task of keeping her safe from devastating feelings, thoughts and memories.

Her wish to not know, to forget, was manifested by frequent episodes of forgetting events in her life. Appointments were mixed up or missed, names of restaurants were misremembered; occurrences that happened between sessions were placed out of awareness, dreams and thoughts forgotten. This symptom reflected her fervent desire to forget; to forget in the present allowed her to break the link with the painful past.

Recently she went on a trip with a friend, a frequent travel companion who decided for the first time to bring her husband along. After the trip, Maggie was stunned by the dysfunction of their marriage, dismayed by their constant squabbling. Her surprise was a bit surprising, as Maggie had previously witnessed first hand the marital strife. But being in close proximity stimulated other issues, ones that she had ample reason to "forget."

Maggie was bewildered by the endless bickering and by the intensity and meanness expressed. It seemed way too much, and she couldn't understand her friends' degree of dysfunction as well as her level of distress. I told her that I thought that the close quarters might have brought up some sexual tension. After I mentioned that idea, Maggie was incredulous, "On what did you base that on?" I told her that I just wondered about it, since other reactions to her beauty had tended to be problematic. She then *remembered* that her friend's husband jokingly commented to the proprietor of the rental property about his "two wives." Maggie further told me that she and the woman shared a bed, allegedly because the husband couldn't tolerate his wife's snoring. A situation rife for conflict, I thought. And we wondered why Maggie was so surprised, since she knew the quality of their relationship, and since there was ample past evidence to at least consider a sexually based tension (Maggie's friend had made snide and presumably jealous comments about Maggie's attractiveness in the past). Maggie disavowed because it was too close to her history where her father's sexual interest in her was not only terribly frightening and confusing, but also interfered with her relationship with her mother. Although she did nothing to evoke these feelings in past or present, she feared being responsible. As this was not new material, it didn't take us long to understand the origins of her discomfort, and she was soon able to feel more relaxed and less threatened.

Maggie's therapy helped her to connect past and present by addressing long-repressed memories and affects occasioned by the traumas of childhood. Her strengthened ego capacity allowed her to more smoothly process affects. Similar conflicts arise as in the past but she can now cope with the adversity much more effectively.

Constructions and Reconstructions

As I described in the previous chapter, we are always limited by our own subjectivity; it is impossible to assert that we have attained some "truth" about external experience, or memory. The process of therapy is not designed to diminish conflict by finding the "truth" as to the origins of a problematic relationship, but to find a way to conceptualize outer experiences and inner feeling states in a way that feels right to the parties involved, fits in with what is known about the individual's character structure, and appears to match a consensual view of reality.

Sandler and Sandler (1992) differentiate between the actions of construction and reconstruction within the psychotherapeutic process:

> Constructions provide an organized framework for the patient's knowledge of how he functions, consciously and unconsciously, in the present, while reconstructions provide the patient with a temporal dimension to his understanding of himself, a developmental perspective which allows him to perceive and to tolerate the previously unaccepted 'child within.' Constructions and reconstructions can come to form an organized frame of reference for the patient's inner world, including the patterns of relationship between the self and the structures we call internal objects. Constructions and reconstructions, like all structures of insight, may in the course of time function for the most part unconsciously. (47)

In thinking of character structure having a consistency over time, how one conceptualizes, feels and places events within the psyche should have coherence. That is, the consistency of character structure is such that a person will process events, feelings and thoughts similarly past and present (allowing for changes from development, and difference in circumstance). We can see that Maggie handles affects in a way that is consistent from past to present. The work of the therapy is to help her gain understanding of her present-day functioning, including unconscious mechanisms, and to gain understanding of the factors (memories) that have been forgotten from the past that, despite forgotten, have affected her functioning. Sandler and Sandler (1984) refer to these aspects of unconscious functioning as the "present unconscious" and the "past unconscious" respectively. The Sandlers' advocate the advisability of attending to both past and present unconscious systems (more about their conceptions in the final two chapters).

Dangers in Remembering

There are caveats as to the desirability of maintaining a goal of memory reconstruction. First, one must always respect the psyche's need for defense, and a therapist who is insistent on a patient remembering can create too much anxiety culminating in the patient either becoming more symptomatic or fleeing. And sometimes efforts toward memory reconstruction obscure what is transpiring in the moment between therapist and patient. It is always important to remember that any psychic activity can be used for defense, as when a jump to the past is designed to avoid the feelings in the present.

And then there are those whose traumatic history is so intense that memory reconstruction can be retraumatizing. Auerhahn and Laub (1998) point out that some trauma (in their reference to Holocaust survivors) is so severe that it has not been processed symbolically and thus is not accessible to memory reconstruction, and an attempt to recapture memories can excite extreme emotions triggering psychic fragmentation and fears of ego dissolution.

Fantasies

Everyone has fantasies, conscious and otherwise. Fantasies can be pleasant, creating intense feelings of happiness and contentment or can be frightening like the worst nightmare. Like dreams (Freud, 1900) fantasies often have a wish fulfilling aspect even when that is not readily apparent.

My patient Emma, as a child, had a recurring fantasy that her parents would somehow leave her or die while she was still a child and this fantasy felt strongly alluring despite the obvious painful content. When we discussed it, she felt that it had to do with intense feelings about separation. I wasn't so sure but couldn't come up with a better explanation. At a later time in the therapy, we were discussing some of her intense possessive desires toward me and that the fact that others in my family were, "more important" than her was so hurtful. After expressing these thoughts and feelings, she would immediately tell herself she was silly, bringing the "reality" (that of course I would have others in my life, etc.) of the circumstance center ground. She recalled her old fantasy, thinking it had something to do with these topics. At this point I felt that I understood the dynamic better. I told her that the fantasy served the function of consciously negating the "reality" of her situation within her family. That is, she had felt that she had already "lost" her parents to her dreaded rival sister who was only fourteen months older. The fantasy defended against the conscious awareness of her anger and hurt by the reality of her parents' love for her sister (and the loss of love that she felt) by substituting a less likely scenario—the death of parents at her early age. Similarly by telling herself that she was silly about her feelings toward me she was negating the vigor of her feelings—that she wasn't really *that* upset about the nature of our relationship (which of course does not mean that I didn't feel affection and attachment to her). In this regard the fantasy of being my one true love is defended against by the "reality" of our relationship.

Fantasy production is a source of richness and creativity. In life and in psychotherapy, it should not be discouraged, but rather elaborated and enhanced, for pleasure and as a clear window into the psyche, as with Emma. Oftentimes fantasies, when deconstructed, provide valuable information to patient and therapist toward understanding more of the mind of the patient, and what might be transpiring in the therapeutic relationship. In other words, individuals may turn to dreams or fantasies to express wishes and conflicts that are not consciously available for discussion. Emma's insistence on "reality" was a clear indication of her intense and insistent feelings about our relationship. Or, as James tells me about a daydream about doing something heroic. There are many possible motivating factors for the development of the fantasy. But some of them may relate to feelings about me—that he wishes I thought he was heroic, that he feels that I am, that he is uncomfortable with feelings or thoughts about himself or me and would rather that we were heroes than scoundrels, as examples. At different times in the therapy, any or all of these scenarios can be operational, and understanding and elaborating them is very beneficial toward understanding conflict and fantasies that serve to defend against the awareness of what feel to be untenable feelings of conflict.

Central Fantasies

In the process of growing up, children often feel frustrated both by expected hurts encountered in the family constellation and by the humiliations suffered by the child's awareness of his physical and intellectual "inferiority," that is, inferior in contrast to an adult. Add to these psychic injuries those that are greater than expected (traumatic) and children can feel overcome and overwhelmed by feelings of helplessness and incompetence. As compensation children develop fantasies that serve to salve hurts and humiliations. These fantasies can be conscious and used by children for soothing, but often times they reside in nonconscious levels. As the child matures, central fantasies often move underground but some adults still use fantasies as "bedtime stories" to calm the turbulent psychic waters. Even when the fantasy is conscious, the significance and unconscious roots remain hidden. Some of these fantasies coalesce into enduring ones, central fantasies that give shape to one's character structure.

These fantasies have several qualities in common. First of all, the central character is seen if not heroic, then at least shown in a positive light, although this may be disguised. Secondly the fantasy allows for an imagined satisfaction of hidden wishes and desires. Thirdly, the fantasy neatly takes care of reality constraints. And finally the fantasy absolves the individual of guilt or shame, or finds a more acceptable mode of disposal of these unpleasant affects. The central fantasies are elaborated compromise formations (Brenner, 1982) that contain the same elements of wishes being satisfied, reality problems managed, and guilt absolved. Many symptoms can be considered as manifestations of compromise formations. Awareness of the central fantasy can serve as a therapeutic touchstone, providing a context from which further understandings and interpretations can emerge.

Let's look at Maggie's central fantasy and contrasting central anxiety. In growing up Maggie was subjected to a number of traumas and deprivations. Her brother drowned when she was nine, her mother was unmercifully cruel and hateful, her father sexually inappropriate—all in all an atmosphere of much too much. As a response to this, Maggie developed her cool, calm and collected demeanor as a defense against uncomfortable, overwhelming, frightening and forbidden thoughts and feelings, a response to the too much. This became her mode of being that developed out of implicit, explicit and atmospheric memories, and became an important part of her character structure. Her central fantasy consisted of seeing herself impervious to emotional turmoil. In this fantasy she feels no anger and no guilt—she is absolutely clean and neat. Wishes become minimized and she concentrates on solving interpersonal problems through denial and self-abnegation (think of her encounter with Gloria). By denying so much pleasure to herself, including release of aggression, she can feel morally clean, as self-denial and absence of aggression are so valued. Although the fantasy seems to handle overt anxiety and distress, it does not provide sufficient flexibility to deal with emotionally vibrant situations. When these occur, her central anxiety becomes activated and she begins to feel overwhelmed and immeasurably anxious.

Let's go back to my schema of a central fantasy. First, *Maggie as heroic*: Maggie casts herself in a blameless light. As a denier of pleasure and purveyor of interpersonal sacrifice (she almost always places others' needs or wishes ahead of her own), Maggie places herself in a position where she is beyond reproach. Second, *the central fantasy as a vehicle toward satisfaction of wishes*: Maggie, like all of us, has many needs, most of which are denied, though. That which is avoided is avoided for a reason. Maggie's aggression, more problematic because it feels so dangerous, comes to be felt even more intensely and in turn requires ever more strenuous defenses. Needs for nurturance are also subject to defensive maneuvers because her history of abuse makes her feel vulnerable when needful. These affects become "satisfied" in two ways. When aggression becomes activated, it is immediately denied (unconsciously) and turned into self-criticism or self-sacrifice. The hostility is gratified in a self-destructive fashion. Her needs for nurturance also become satisfied when they are projected onto others. For instance she would nurture and oversupply her very needy sister, denying her own needs (and her aggression) for love and affection and feeling gratified vicariously by giving to her sister. Third, *reality constraints dealt with:* Valued by friends and employers for her selflessness, she was always in their good graces and earned many rewards as an employee, gratifying her sense of value and reinforcing the self-sacrifice, and reinforcing to her that she was "really" helpful and not destructive. Finally, *consideration of guilt:* Her selflessness and self-denial also enabled her to not feel guilty for her less than positive feelings toward her sister, for instance.

Her fantasy was a solution to the untenable childhood situation of too much aggression, too much sexuality, too many boundaries violated, too much neglect and too much guilt. It was the therapeutic goal to help her to understand that the central fantasy provided an *illusion* of safety, and that its inflexibility actually opened her to great anxiety. In large part, our therapy consisted of us trying to help her to identify and discuss defended-against affects that felt dangerous and forbidden. All of this operated toward the ultimate goal of assisting her to work through and to render her internal conflicts less dangerous.

Central Themes

Central fantasies can evolve into central themes; themes coalesce from the aggregates of wishes, desires and prohibitions. These "organizing strands," as Klein (1998) has named them, are akin to a theme in a novel, a unifying idea that when identified, provides a sense of substance and meaningfulness to both patient and therapist. Others have written in this area as well. In similar fashion, Lachmann and Lichtenberg (1992) refer to "model scenes," Weiss and Sampson (1986) to "pathogenic beliefs" and Luborsky (1984) to "core conflictual relationship themes."

It is often useful to discuss "themes" as opposed to fantasies, particularly early in the treatment when it is harder for patients to accept a mind that can function without conscious awareness, a mind that has not only conscious fantasies and other attributes, but a mind unknown, and that which is unknown is often felt to be ominous.

For example, when Marie spoke about her anxiety and distress in watching *Madagascar 2*, I first interpreted her distress as related to her parents' shaming responses to her spontaneity. When I connect the anxiety while watching the movie to a theme, Marie can more viscerally understand how this issue has compromised her sense of freedom of action, thought and feeling throughout her life. These interpretations are experience—near, easily comprehended and less threatening than speaking about unconscious wishes that may involve forbidden feelings of hostility, for example.

Concluding Thoughts

In my continuing discussion about conflict, I have highlighted three aspects of the psyche in this chapter. The first has to do with levels of consciousness and I demonstrated how these aspects could be understood in terms of conflicts. The second has to do with central fantasies and corresponding anxieties. The third is to look at remembering and forgetting, and the centrality of recapturing memory is in working toward conflict resolution.

It's not news to experienced psychotherapists how "sticky" patient symptoms seem, and resistant to change. An understanding of central fantasies, and how they often reflect unremembered aspects of life, can assist one in understanding the compelling quality of an individual's behavior, and how and why conflict arises.

My focus is now shifting from more general considerations of how personality is formed toward a description of more specific aspects, such as how internal conflicts affect the ability to use one's mind effectively and how conflicts affect the developmental challenges that all of us face.

PART TWO

WHO AM I, AND HOW DID I GET THIS WAY?

Now that I have described some general components of the psyche (character structure, memory systems, central fantasies, levels of consciousness), it is time to look more closely at the development of specific personality characteristics—their idiosyncratic (to the individual in question) formation, within and outside of conflict, and when related to conflict, equally unique techniques of resolution.

All of the features that I have discussed thus far and will further discuss can be deemed as aspects of character structure that offer different "angles" of perspective looking through the character structure "window." In thinking about specific personality characteristics, it is important to remember that personality is incredibly complex and that personality qualities are interwoven with each other, as opposed to operating in isolation. Further complicating this already complex matter is that some of these aspects compete against each other. For instance, let's think about attachment and separation issues. Every individual has attachment needs but at the same time must maintain degrees of separateness and individuality. An individual with separation "issues" has attachment "issues" as well. The dialectic between these two polarities begins in childhood and the manner in which these interpersonal dilemmas are dealt with contributes to relative degrees of emotional health.

Because of the breadth of material in this arena, it makes sense to me to partition the material into three separate chapters. In the first, I will explicate ways in which people configure their cognitive capacities when confronting conflict. Following that, I will range a bit further into other aspects of the psyche that highlight its complexity. Finally I will discuss how individuals are conflicted between their desire to, on one hand, know their minds intricately and intimately and, on the other, to avoid self-awareness for fear of delving into areas scary and forbidden.

CHAPTER FOUR

The Problem-Solving Mind

Even if it does not always seem evident, everyone strives to make good choices when confronting problems of life, to find adaptive solutions to vexing dilemmas. Yet we know that severe conflict interferes with patients' ability to effectively engage their minds in productive fashions.

Individuals vary greatly in their ability to use their intellectual capabilities to effectively solve problems. Some have minds that seem closed and rigid, while others process information and make decisions in a smooth and effective fashion. What are the factors that lead one way or toward the other, and how do they relate to conflictual matters? In this chapter I will be addressing cognitive ability to process conflict from two perspectives: mental flexibility and reflexive function. From there I will move on to discuss methods that individuals develop in order to attempt to create order and safety out of what often feels like chaotic unpredictability.

Mental Flexibility

Individuals come into therapy varying in degrees of "mental flexibility." Some are much more "agile," in that they are able to use their minds effectively to problem solve, to manage affects reasonably effectively, to allow the therapist relatively unencumbered access into their conscious and nonconscious minds, to be introspective, and to make productive moves internally and behaviorally from insights. These individuals have active minds. Others, however, feel more stultified and have blocks toward free association and metaphor. They tend toward more concrete thinking, and either do not allow a freer range of thought or are unable to find the wherewithal to do so. People with these characteristics can be considered to have passive and concrete thinking processes. Childhood experiences mainly determine the degree of mental flexibility although temperament has an effect as well.

With each of the psychic aspects I am discussing, an individual falls somewhere on a continuum. Everyone who comes to a psychotherapist does so because some area of their psyche is not working as effectively as they would like. Part of the psychotherapeutic process with any patient is to promote a more limber mind.

Novick and Novick (2004) and Fairbairn (1958) write about "open" and "closed" minds in terms of development and self-regulation. Although the Novicks are more specific as to the traumatic origins of those who possess more closed minds, both affirm that more severe backgrounds compromise the patient's capability to engage the environment in a more open and flexible way. Here is what the Novicks say about the closed system:

> [It is an] . . . omnipotent sadomasochistic system. We call this the "closed system" because it avoids and denies reality; is unchanging, circular, and repetitive; and is characterized by static omnipotent sadomasochistic modes of functioning. We call the other system the "open system" because it is attuned to inner and outer reality; constantly expands and changes; and is characterized by joy, competence and creativity in self-regulation, problem solving, and conflict resolution. These two systems represent alternative potential responses to developmental challenges, available to anyone from birth on. Even the most disturbed patient has the potential for open-system responses; even the best-analyzed patient never loses the potential for closed-system responses. (brackets added, 238)

Fairbairn points out that patients with "closed" systems are wedded to their internal worlds, and have problems in letting newer relationships (including that with the therapist) replace their more archaic unhealthy identifications. We know that those with traumatic backgrounds have challenges beyond those who come from healthier backgrounds. In this present regard, we see them as having less ability to use their minds to solve problems or manage affects, especially those of anger and aggression; just as the Novicks describe these individuals' proclivity toward sadomasochistic expressions of hostility in conflictual situations, internal and/or external.

I am going to illustrate these concepts using a case history of a patient who had considerable difficulty in using his mind effectively, resulting in poor conflict management. Len, thirty-five, came to me with profound unhappiness. A massive man weighing more than 350 lbs., Len told me that he had always been overweight even though everyone else in his family (two brothers, three sisters and parents) were thin. He described his father as noncommunicative and physically abusive, and there were vague allegations that the father was sexually inappropriate to some, if not all, of the children. Len's mother was severely depressed when he was a child and later received a diagnosis of dissociative identity disorder.

Len's mother recognized his unhappiness early in his childhood. From about eight years on Len has been in one sort of therapy or another. His mother took him to see her therapist, and he saw him until he graduated from high school. After college he saw another psychologist until that clinician retired, and thereupon Len was referred to me. Len was unhappily married, and really didn't know why he married his wife as he professed to never have loved her, and believed that she didn't feel much in the way of positive feelings toward him. He indicated that when deciding to marry he didn't really think about his lack of affection toward his wife and in hindsight wondered whether he married her for fear he couldn't find anyone else. He told me that he felt unsatisfied in his work although he was quite successful in the construction industry. His weight was a constant problem, yet he could not do anything about it even though he wished he could eat better and exercise more. He was perplexed as to many aspects of his functioning—why and whom he married, why he felt so unhappy, why he could not lose weight and why he felt no satisfaction in life. His previous therapies seemed to be minimally helpful, and he appeared to have little insight into the etiology of his psychic distress. I could certainly see that his parents' psychological difficulties must have impacted him, but had trouble finding direct connections in his associations between past and present. Part of the reason for that is that Len had great difficulty in free associating, or in associating at all. Generally he would come into a session and give me a very cursory rundown of the day's events, with next to no detail or emotion about anything save his constant irritation with his wife.

Not only that but he yawned frequently, and the sleepiness was contagious. We discussed this and he informed me that his previous therapist had had the same problem. I later connected this sleepiness with his childhood nighttime experiences when his mother would drowse on the couch in his room while he played in his crib. The lack of interaction between mother and son was telling and disturbing. Interpreting that he and I were reenacting the scenario of two drowsy individuals operating in parallel with next to no interpersonal contact made sense to him but had no emotional impact and the yawning did not diminish. Nothing seemed to get through to him.

This too was discussed, again with no change in behavior. We discussed his difficult background and he would agree that he was probably not wanting to get into painful material (perhaps by trying to put our minds to sleep as a way of keeping us from the exploration of frightening material), but he couldn't find any way to be different, or even a real drive to find a way to use his mind more intensely. What about anger and aggression? Len indicated to me that his most present affect was irritation—at his wife, at his boss, at traffic, and a bit at me (I should mention that he faithfully attended his five times weekly appointments), and at himself. He received little pleasure in life. At times he obtained some gratification from making life miserable for his wife and clearly was self-punitive as well; behaviors in line with the Novicks' ideas on sadomasochism. In some sense, I felt that his sleepiness was an attempt to destroy my ability to think and to use my mind effectively and felt that this was likely, in part, a manifestation of hostility. But any felt rage was well buried and not available to us.

His unhappy wife pressured him to engage in marriage counseling, and he went begrudgingly. As with me he complained about his wife in that therapy but apparently neither he nor his wife could manage to engage in meaningful dialogue about their relationship. Finally agreeing on something, they terminated the counseling and their marriage continued in its usual arid fashion. His motivation to improve his marriage was minimal since he didn't like his wife, didn't want to try to work on it and felt that it was hopeless. Why didn't he divorce? I wondered. He wasn't sure but indicated that he was afraid of the unknown ("the enemy you know . . .") and was concerned about the effect of divorce on his relationship with his two young children. As he was so unhappy and we were so stuck, I wondered whether he might want to pursue a medication evaluation but he declined, again without much elaboration of thought on the matter.

Although this sounds quite dismal, I am pleased to report that Len and I were eventually able to develop a more dynamic therapy. I will save my discussion of that until the chapters on specific therapeutic interventions. But for now, let's now look at the causative factors for his closed psychic system. Len presumably was overwhelmed by stimuli in growing up. An abusive father and a psychologically absent and inconsistent mother left him adrift in a sea of too-intense emotions. Lacking a way to think about what was occurring, Len developed techniques of not thinking. Without more adaptive responses available to him, Len turned to food for solace. Using food to pacify also prevented him from having intense affects.

To his mother's credit, she did seek out treatment for him but it was inadvisable and ineffective for the two to have the same therapist. I suspected that his mother's dissociative disorder made her too distant and inconsistent and that he tenaciously clung to her (both in external terms and in internal representations) for reassurance since he felt her presence to be unreliable. Desperately attached, he was not likely to give his mother up for new objects (and seeing his mother's therapist only reinforced the tie). By marrying someone that he didn't love, he could remain symbolically attached to his original object (mother) and retain the unconscious childhood fantasy of reunion with a "good" mother. Taking in suggestions from me, or establishing a relationship with me would threaten his tenuous tie with mother. Identifying with her dissociative aspects also kept him close to her yet rendered him unable to use his mind in more effective and flexible ways.

I believe that it is correct to say that he was afraid of delving into his mind for fear of becoming in touch with what might have felt like intolerable feelings. But his block in this was also caused by factors beyond defense. His family's implicit way of relating did not favor thoughtful consideration. Rather it modeled abuse and dissociation. He had no "working models" (Bowlby, 1969) of thought that would even put him in the ballpark of careful consideration of his internal world.

What about conflict? Because of the preponderance of unprocessed hostility, Len was trapped by his conflictual feelings. He desired love but was afraid to let go of his internal "safe" object; he feared that a real relationship would be more dangerous (with the possibility of heartbreak and of other hard feelings) than his dearly held unsatisfying but familiar internal one. Guilt over aggressive feelings caused intense self-punitive behavior (obesity, marrying not for love). Forever angry, he was forever not satisfied, providing a venue for expression of anger but never with any sense of closure or pleasure. In other words, conflict was equated with overstimulating aggression and was avoided strenuously. And his "closed" mind provided little help in the way of solving problems.

Reflective Function

Fonagy (1991) has written on reflective function in a paper entitled, "Thinking about Thinking." He describes one's ability to "conceive of conscious and unconscious mental states in oneself and others as the capacity to mentalize" (641). A patient with an active mind can use his/her mind to contemplate before acting, to understand the difference between one's own wishes and that of another, to understand boundaries between self and other, to be able to respond to feedback when given in an appropriate fashion, can recognize distortions when pointed out; in essence to be able to *reflect*.

Many, many individuals suffer from a defect in this reflective function, most likely a result of over or understimulating childhood experience. As Fonagy puts it,

> The parents' abuse undermines the child's theory of mind, so that it is no longer safe for the child, for example, to think about wishing, if this implies the contemplation of the all too real wishes of the parent to harm the child. The secondary representation of mental events may thus become permanently inhibited. Such inhibition may turn out to have substantial benefits for the individual because it enables him to circumvent intolerable psychic pain. Individuals whose primary objects are unloving and cruel may find the contemplation of the contents of the mind of the object unbearable. (650)

We can see the direct relevance of this with Len. Unbearable thoughts of his parents' abuse and neglect interfered with his ability to reflect upon difficult issues. The apparent reality of his then girlfriend's lack of affection and love (he had informed me of many hurtful actions by his wife prior to their marriage) was too painful to contemplate as it likely reminded him of his parents' actions and feelings, and he was unable to break off the relationship despite many provocations. He could only see bleakness and despair should he end up not married, and could not forecast that he could use his interpersonal and cognitive abilities to forge a better life.

Consistent with Fonagy's ideas, Len's reflective function was impaired. If, for example, I would ask Len how he experienced my absence when I was on vacation, Len would describe what he did in the time I was away. Asked if he had any feelings about it, he would often respond by telling me that he "felt everyone needed a vacation," and when I pointed out that what he said wasn't really a feeling, he was perplexed. As another example: he might describe an altercation with his wife and couldn't really point to any affects other than irritation, and if I asked for elaboration, he repeated himself several times indicating the he was irritated. And although I was quite sure that his rendition of his wife's behavior had a least some semblance of reality, I also didn't think he was the easiest man to live with either. But I sensed no empathy or even sympathy toward his wife. This is another aspect of a defect in reflective function, as he couldn't allow himself to reflect upon another's affective world.

Conflicts with others and internal conflicts (related to his need to overeat and his contradictory wish to be in shape, for instance) were not only not resolved; options and strategies for conflict resolution didn't even enter his mind. The world of thought and feelings was dangerous and not available for him to use to navigate the world effectively, and this includes not being able to, in any way, ponder his contributions to the marital distress, or to even talk to his wife in an understandable way of his objections to her behaviors. The same applied to his overeating—he wanted to be in better shape but would have difficulty in identifying triggers to his overeating or even to "remember" (i.e., think about) to make an effort to limit his food intake.

Despite our difficulties Len very much wanted to get better but, in the early years of treatment, couldn't see his way to healthier functioning. I will address some of the reasons for this common quandary in the next section.

The Adaptive Mind

Every symptom, as painful as it might be, and as desperate as a person is not to be burdened by it, is an attempt to salvage some satisfaction and esteem from what was originally an even worse state of affairs. The manner in which an individual configures his life is done so in order to psychically persist under internal and external stresses. That this effort is not always successful in managing pain is salient and is the reason one seeks out treatment, but the fact remains that these symptoms are attempts to adapt to pressures and represent a bulwark against even more painful affects. Len despaired of ever finding anyone who could love him. Staying with his wife was a compromise; he wasn't alone (which he greatly feared), he could retain ties with his internalized mother, he could find avenues of punishment for inner feelings of badness, and he could gain some satisfaction because of his elevation of suffering to a virtue. This is an adaptation to what felt like untenable psychic conflicts.

Here's another example. Maggie led a life that, on the surface, seemed sublimely peaceful. Her house was clean and orderly, she was always neatly dressed, and she never had a bad word to say about anyone. She appeared calm, cool and collected. Despite these outward appearances, she continuously warded off anxiety for fear that she would feel too much and become overwhelmed by "chaos." Early in treatment she felt threatened by what she referred to as "losing her mental health" and later on felt her affects to be intolerably messy and shameful. What are the origins for this? Past and present have strong concordance, i.e., past events have influenced her feelings about herself in the present. In childhood, her father demanded that the house be kept impeccably clean and berated her mother for what he felt was shoddy housekeeping. And she remembered when her mother exclaimed in disgust when cleaning her baby brother's dirty diapers and also recalled her mother's rage over her brother's fecal play. But these are just some explicit examples of her parents' emotional disorders. In general strong feelings, behaviors or what her parents considered aberrant thoughts were indications of essential badness and Maggie connected this sense of badness with shameful fecal incontinence. Hypercriticalness made her hypersensitive over thoughts, feelings or actions that had any degree of intensity, and she associated these psychic entities as being fraught, dirty and dangerous.

Her orderliness kept her internal critical faculty (internalized from her parents) and frightening thrusts toward aggression at bay, and in doing so helped her to maintain a sense of calm despite the volcanic nature of her affects. In addition, her traumatic experiences created a profound sense of being unsafe—from her own feelings and from those of others. Being so capable and calm allowed her to feel less at risk.

Without a working model of effective affect management from childhood and in order to function at a level of competence and calm, Maggie needed to come up with a way to not be derailed by the intensity of her affects. Using her formidable intelligence, Maggie developed compartmentalizing techniques to keep "dirty" feelings out of awareness and this, throughout her life, allowed her to successfully complete her education, to be an excellent and dedicated employee, and to be able to maintain her life without impinging negatively on others. This was her adaptive response to affects and thoughts that felt dangerous and forbidden. Unfortunately, though, her solution of maintaining cleanliness and order was unstable and fragile and did not really protect her from feeling overwhelmed when confronted with intense affects. Further, her need to keep feelings submerged affected the course of therapy since she could not allow herself to "play" (Fonagy and Target, 1996) with ideas and fantasies. Further still, the stiffness of her defenses affected emotional flexibility, limiting her ability to solve conflicts productively. Adaptations are types of "Faustian" bargains, designed to reduce discomfort on one hand but resulting in a reduction of effective functioning on the other.

In the next several sections, I will elaborate on other ways in which the mind develops adaptive solutions to conflict.

Turning a Trauma into a Triumph

Trauma profoundly disables. Many others (Krystal, 1988; Herman, 1992; van der Kolk, 1987, to name a few) and I (Hooberman, 2002, 2007) have written on the devastating effects of trauma. The literature on the subject is vast; thus I won't even attempt to review that which has been written, and nor will I delve into a discussion of many of the ramifications of abuse. I will concentrate on how those who have been traumatized attempt to make the best of horrible situations, i.e., to adapt to them.

Lisa, age thirty-five, was referred to me for more in-depth treatment by the eating disorder clinic that she had attended for treatment of anorexia. At the point of referral, Lisa had been erratic in maintaining healthy eating and was prone to deep depression. She had been prescribed a variety of antidepressant and mood stabilizing medications without receiving sufficient benefit. Lisa was frustrated by her inability to move to more enduring health. She told me that she restricted her eating not for body image reasons but often in a response to conflict. In other words, she used eating, or rather not eating, to manage affects. She also indicated that she felt proud for not succumbing to hunger. This dynamic would eventually become so satisfying that it had an addictive quality (see below for more discussion of affective addiction).

In our initial meetings I was struck by the quality of our discourse. In reaction to her description of the events of the day, or of something troubling, I might say something to her that I thought might be illuminating. And usually her response was to smilingly nod, without further elaboration. I couldn't figure out if she was being polite, if she was already cognizant of what I was trying to interpret or something else. I asked her about it and she couldn't really provide an explanation either. I spoke with her psychologist from the anorexia clinic and she also knew what I meant but was at a loss as well. To me this behavior felt quite withholding, somewhat "stingy," and perhaps imperious.

Lisa told me more of her life history. Diagnosed with a hip deformity as an infant, she was placed in full body casting with a bar separating her legs. She was also found to have a mitral valve prolapse that required frequent monitoring, which later in childhood hobbled her ability to be as physically active as she would have liked. Lisa described a very difficult past life with her parents. Her father was authoritarian and volatile, especially around the dinner table. Mother was seriously depressed and had a history of family sexual abuse. Lisa grew up with no real supports and spent much of her childhood frightened and overwhelmed. A bad situation was made even worse by a date rape at age seventeen. Her life was infused with a scarcity of nurturance and an overabundance of hostility and negativity.

Not surprisingly, Lisa's demeanor was quite sour and negative. She took little pleasure in life, including from her immediate family even though she indicated that she loved her husband and children. Bitterly indicting her parents for her mistreatment and their misattunement, she was not about to forgive them, nor was she able to move beyond the configuration of hostile and negative interchanges with her parents, or with those in her contemporary life. In fact her referral to me from the eating disorders clinic appeared to derive, in part, from her therapist's exasperation with what felt like Lisa's stubborn refusal to let go of her ever-present grievances.

After listening to her story and from our reactions to each other, I felt that I had a sense of the meaning of her symptoms. I suggested to her that the dismissive stance that she took with me (and I thought with others as well) was firstly an attempt to keep people at a distance, which made some sense since people in her life had often been so hurtful. But perhaps even more importantly, it was also an attempt to both maintain self-esteem and express aggression. Being physically restricted as an infant and emotionally restricted throughout her childhood, she had adopted what had been traumatic and transformed it into something that felt triumphant. That is, whenever she experienced uncomfortable affects, she would withdraw emotional contact with others (restricting them from her involvement) and would restrict her eating and become noncommunicative. She would then feel superiority over those who she had frustrated in the face of her intransigence. In essence she now turned the tables on "tormentors" and no longer felt the victim, but now she was on top of the world. Denying her need for hunger represented a denial of need for any kind of nurturance or sustenance and she looked down upon those who could not use the same kind of self-denial. She saw all of her maneuvers as strengths, not as weaknesses.

From the childhood position of being powerless and not in control of her physical and psychic selves (her tragedy), Lisa developed a solution that felt more satisfying. Restricting became her prevalent mode of affect management in that it managed emotions that felt dangerous and forbidden. It also provided her with an opportunity to indirectly express her anger; to monumentally frustrate others while maintaining a stance of supremacy. These conflict management techniques created a sense of satisfaction (her triumph) and were better than feeling helpless and victimized, and in that sense they were adaptive. Yet they did not really lead toward enduring and healthy satisfaction of needs or of fruitful resolution of conflicts.

This configuration of "turning tragedy into triumph" is quite common amongst those with severe backgrounds and can be difficult to overcome since it is so effective in minimizing deep despair and achieving some stability and satisfaction. As with all of these configurations, I will address treatment later on.

The Addictive Mind

Any psychic activity can be addictive. Anxiety, as bad as it is, can feel better than despair, for instance. Frequent occurrences of anxiety create what may be called psychic "ruts" which entice those who, with limited psychic resources, are confronting complex emotional interactions. Joyce, discussed in the first chapter, was like that. She had been raised in an atmosphere of recrimination and hopelessness. She withered from her parents' constant criticism. Anxiety became a constant companion that eventually became an ally, "an old friend," as she put it, and like all good friends difficult to give up. This is no different than how an alcoholic feels about her cocktails, a smoker about his cigarettes, an obese person about his French fries, or how Lisa felt about restricting behaviors. There is a seduction in compulsivity. The anxiety in Joyce's case, or the restriction for Lisa, or any other compulsive behavior, has several compelling qualities. The behavior feels familiar, it has psychic organizing aspects (one feels more secure in the "rut" than metaphorically careening wildly across the landscape), seems to be more under the person's control and enables the person to grab some pleasure in the midst of painful and despairing feelings. The addiction substitutes compulsive, repetitive behavior for affects that may feel overpowering. In this it is adaptive but of course limiting in that the person in question does not have the flexibility to solve conflicts more productively. And, of course the addictions have problems of their own, serving the often unconscious need for punishment.

"All I Need to Know I Learned in Kindergarten"[1]

Robert Fulghum (1988), in his very popular book, points out that many of the learnings achieved in kindergarten such as "share everything" and "play fair" are concepts that stand in good stead throughout life. Good points to be sure. Yet there are ways in which individuals have not been able to transcend simple truisms to more complexities of thought. These unfortunate individuals continue to follow what may be unsupported beliefs through the rest of their lives. I say unfortunate because those with this disposition have trouble learning from experience and instead follow an aphorism that might read, "If I believe it, it must be true." Britton (1995) describes how patients with these narcissistic pathologies concretize their early childhood developed beliefs into what they insist are "knowledge." Ferociously wedded to these anxiety-relieving beliefs, these patients can be very difficult to treat. If one is certain about complex matters, life seems much simpler and less scary, and for those who have been traumatized this is a bargain hard to resist. I am aware that everyone's pathology contains certainties about reality (psychic reality) that are somewhat impervious to adult experience. Yet the individuals that I am presently describing are far more insistent on the rightness of their beliefs as well as rigid in their certainty. Again this adaptation is better than overwhelming anxiety and self-hatred, but it compromises healthy functioning because of the individual's impaired ability to learn from experience.

Here is an example: Kevin, age forty-nine, came to me with what he described as unremitting marital difficulties. He indicated that he loved his wife Linda but couldn't get over her "faults." I was sure that Linda had her own problems but Kevin's complaints about her seemed a bit picky and obsessive. For instance, he insisted that his wife make the beds in the same fashion as his mother did. Never mind that he didn't see this as a shared responsibility, Kevin couldn't move beyond his childhood conception of the "rightness" of his mother's bed-making techniques. When queried he indicated that there are "right ways of doing things and . . ." When he and his wife would quarrel he would take the same stance, insist that he was right without considering her point of view. He told me that others had told him that he was a bit of a "know it all" and I could see that since he often made sweeping pronouncements about human behavior. I knew that this originated from insecurity but, like others, found this to be a bit irritating. I raised this with him and he embarrassedly acknowledged that he knew that his attitudes could be a bit much but felt he "couldn't help himself." He also intellectually realized that this was generated from anxiety.

In an association to this, he told me a story about his mother serving a cherry pie at a holiday dinner. She couldn't find canned cherries (without sugar) as the recipe called for so substituted cherries in sugared syrup. Yet she didn't adjust the recipe for the added sugar in the can, resulting in a pie that he said had so much sugar that it, "made my teeth hurt." Having similar dynamics as he did, Kevin's mother felt she had to follow the rules of the recipe and couldn't productively use her mind to come up with a more reasonable and healthy alternative (adjust the sugar accordingly). Instead she followed the dictates set down by *her* mother, to wit: always follow the rules (no matter how ridiculous they may be). Correspondingly, Kevin followed his mother's rules without consideration. To do otherwise challenged the order of his internal world and would cause anxiety should he venture from the family way of doing business. This too was adaptive, in that it kept him in concert with his internally critical mother but was detrimental as it interfered with his relationship with his wife, as well as preventing him from thinking creatively in other areas of his life.

Kevin learned very early on in life (in kindergarten age or before) that his best strategy in keeping safe was to go along with the dictates set down by his mother. To do otherwise would invite criticism and derision. The underlying fear of humiliation and shame kept him locked into belief systems that were rigid and unyielding and not subject to experience. This interfered with our therapy since my job as therapist was to question unsupported beliefs. Kevin never saw these as questions but as challenges, which had to be refuted in order to maintain his sense of order in the world and to stave off the humiliation of being "wrong." His need to bolster his shaky self-esteem trumped any desire for insight into his dynamics. This point of view is obviously not optimal for problem solving or conflict resolution. One goal in the therapy was for Kevin to realize that "everything he had learned in kindergarten" was not necessarily still applicable in the more complex world of adult activities and relationships, and kept him tied to his early attachment object—his mother.

Control vs. Helplessness

It is not uncommon to hear a person being described as "controlling" and to be sure, this is not meant as a compliment. But let's wonder about this, and contemplate what it means to be "controlling"—controlling what, whom? Those who we find as "controlling" are those who grew up not feeling sufficiently in control of their own mind, body, thoughts, feelings and/or actions. Not everyone with this configuration comes from severe backgrounds; but those who exhibit this trait typically had parents who were "controlling" in their own right, not allowing the child to feel competent in her ability to effectively make choices. Without this degree of confidence, these individuals substitute rules for freedom of choice. As adults, they also do not feel that others (their children, for example) can make correct choices for themselves, or can productively learn from potential errors and as parents, for instance, convey anxiety in many fairly benign situations. The children then become dominated by their parents' anxiety, internalize this dynamic and the cycle continues into the next generation.

"Controlling" people don't control for the sake of control. They are controlling in order to not feel helpless and overwhelmed by anxiety. The anxiety is often generated by concern over the expression of underlying impulses and affects. Controlling people can seem to be motivated by hostility, and can become hostile when they don't get their way but the controlling behavior is more motivated by anxiety than aggression. An example: Patients of all stripes—not just those with mental health problems—are often reluctant to take medication as described and can become hostile in their refusal. This is often a control issue—the individual feels undone by their powerlessness over their condition and think they "don't really need the medication" or "missing a few times won't matter," etc. These rationalizations enable the patient to feel some semblance of control over that which is uncontrollable (one's health).

Again, the intense need to control is an adaptive response to anxiety. Unfortunately it ties the person to her anxiety and limits one's repertoire of responses to situations. Its irritating aspect compromises relationships. And when "likes" attract, explosions can result. It's hard enough to cope with one person who is fearful about losing control, let alone with both participants.

Effects vs. Intention

Young children have difficulty in discerning cause and effect. An untoward event occurs and the child might very well feel that it happened out of intent (Lichtenberg, 2005). I referred to this in chapter 2 as an "attribution error." Overly severe upbringings reinforce this error and the child might grow up believing that "bad" things happen either because of others' malevolence or because of inner "badness" of the child. It is very difficult going through life either feeling victimized or intensely self-critical, and these patients suffer quite a bit. Yet, this configuration makes therapeutic work difficult since the patient tends to either feel blamed or intensely self-critical when interpretations are made concerning the causality of events or behavior (patients can feel "blamed" for their feelings, thoughts or behaviors). Melanie Klein (1946) referred to those mired in this way of thinking as being in the "paranoid position" and this phrase captures the suspiciousness and precariousness that these individuals experience.

My patient Sophie had been sexually and physically abused as a child. At times she struggled to discern causes for friends' behaviors toward her, just as she tried to understand the reasons for her parents' unconscionable behaviors. She could feel enraged at what felt like her friends' mistreatment, yet this would alternate with intense self-hate as she later felt that her friends had ample reasons to hate her. From my perspective, neither of these extremes was accurate. Rather, it seemed to me that because of her sensitivity her friends often were wary of offending her and tended to tread carefully, and she would misread this as disinterest instead of as sensitivity to her sensitivities. Also, of course, her friends, like everyone, had quirks of their own, which I am sure were irksome. But Sophie experienced these quirks as if they were personally directed. The complexity of relationships would confuse her; she preferred to see others and herself in black and white terms. Either they were victimizing her or she deserved being treated poorly because of her essential "badness." In other words, the discomfort that she felt (the effect) was attributed to others' bad motives (their intentions). The narrowness and concreteness of this dynamic does not allow more sophisticated understanding of the complexity of her and of others' psychologies and limit her repertoire of responses under emotional stimulation.

The effect vs. intention dynamic is a developmental challenge that most children are able to overcome but has remained active in Sophie because of the fixating consequences of trauma. Further, it is clear that Sophie's reactions are consonant with the behavior of her parents as they tended to misattribute blame with abandon. Where is the adaptation in this dynamic? This configuration, like all of those mentioned previously, are examples of how the psyche tries to make the best of bad situations. This one follows that dictum but the pain is not mitigated as much as with other adaptive "solutions." Because of the destabilizing effects of trauma, victims struggle to maintain equanimity and often have a pull to withdraw from others. Yet when one is in the "paranoid position," relationships are still active, even though distorted, which is better than interpersonal and emotional isolation. And the rage (directed outward or inward), is emotionally arousing and is "better" than either psychic dissolution or utter despair. Nevertheless, those caught in the throes of the "they hate me, I hate me" dynamic are in excruciating pain and, in severe cases, are prone to suicidality.

Concluding Thoughts

At times individuals are able to use their internal resources productively. But in times of stress, every individual falls back upon her paradigmatic internal structure for conflict resolution. When the internal world is too fraught with intense conflict, the child is overwhelmed and what had been adaptive as a child becomes maladaptive for the adult and eventually interferes with the use of one's mind for effective and efficient conflict resolution. Next I look at more aspects of personality that make their mark on the ability of the patient to effectively process conflict.

Note

1. With apologies to Robert Fulghum.

CHAPTER FIVE

The Complex Mind

Efficacy vs. Incompetence

Human development proceeds from an initial position of utter helplessness and moves toward increasing degrees of independence and self-reliance. A developmental task for each child is to gradually move from a place of relative "ineptitude" to one of increased sense of competence and pleasure in her ability to effectively navigate in the world. It is crucial that parents emotionally respond to the child's need for self-assertion yet recognize the limitations of the youngster's mind and body.

If the parents encourage the child's burgeoning desire to use her mind and body in independent activities, the child develops a sense of competence and trust in being able to solve problems and gain satisfaction through physical and mental activities. At the same time, parents also need to remain available when the child inevitably needs reassurance and comfort; in other words when the little one needs to "surrender" or to "give in" to regressive pulls—to allow herself the pleasure of "letting go"—a nonshameful recognition of her need to regroup (Ghent, 1990). Sensitive parents appreciate the backward and forward movement of progression and necessary retreat. The healthy child feels little discomfort for her neediness, recognizing intuitively that the battle for self-reliance can be exhausting and that refueling needs (Mahler, 1975) are nothing to be ashamed of and represent a healthy accommodation to reality. The child does not feel "inept"; in the recognition of competence feels proud of her burgeoning ability to have an effect on her world, and her nonshameful awareness of needfulness enables her to turn to others for sustenance.

Healthy parents convey to the child that they hear her desires and wish to satisfy them, within reason. In the best of circumstances, frustrations are held to a minimum if possible, but not eliminated. Satisfaction of every whim and wish would result in the child being overindulged and feeling omnipotent. Overindulgence also short-circuits the development and pleasure of problem solving. Reasonable satisfaction of the child's wishes while affording privacy and time to work out problems on her own lead toward a good mixture of assertion and self-reliance on one hand, and an ability to ask for assistance without self-blame or demandingness on the other. The responsiveness of parents to wishes becomes generalized, creating a sense that the child can manage her environment. She feels effective and confident. A child who is the beneficial recipient of such care taking does not feel undone by conflict; rather, she implicitly has confidence in her ability to effectively work toward solutions, and takes pleasure in all of this.

On the other side: a child whose parents who have been insensitive to necessary ebbs and flows of development has more difficulty in developing a realistic appreciation for abilities and limitations. Some parents have the unhappy proclivity toward shaming when a child is unable to maintain previously attained developmental milestones. And in other unfortunate situations, some parents expect far too much from their children and rather than salve the child's frustration over inevitable failures project disappointment. A child raised in these circumstances is prone to senses of inadequacy and shame when confronting trying situations, and the original sense of "ineptitude" follows into later childhood and adulthood. A child with shaming parents has a paucity of problem-solving skills and instead may become unduly anxious and overwhelmed by conflict, in fearing shame and recrimination.

Parents who are inattentive and neglectful leave their child bewildered and overwhelmed by overstimulating conflictual situations. These children try to overcompensate for their anxiety by imagining that they are more competent than they really are. Sometimes they engage in self-defeating or overindulging behaviors (substance abuse is one possible example) or they may develop omnipotent fantasies and find themselves in situations beyond their abilities to cope. Or, absent of problem-solving skills, they can become prone to panic with a rush to quick and often ill-considered solutions to dilemmas. The child replicates parental neglect through self-neglect, and ends up feeling helpless, hopeless and ineffectual, fueling in turn more disastrous acting out.

Let's look at case examples of both helpful and nonhelpful parent-child interactions that affect the child's sense of efficacy. First the nonhelpful: Marie, as I have mentioned, was a stellar soccer player, until she reached the later grades in high school. She initially played on the varsity in ninth grade but as time went on garnered less and less playing time. Marie felt frustrated by this but blamed no one but herself. "I kept choking in games!" she exclaimed with distress. I asked for more associations. She recalled her father's "disgust" with her play. This memory led to further ones; of her father castigating her for not performing as well as he had wished, of her mother criticizing her everyday choices and personal preferences, and of neither parent praising her for various activities or even of positive physical and personality attributes. Our present-day reconstruction suggested that Marie's poor play in high school was due to her being overcome by anxiety—anxiety over failure, anxiety over her angry feelings toward her parents, and anxiety over the nefarious "crime" of being independent and having her own mind. In other words, the conflictual feelings were too much and she "choked" in her distress. Her ability to be effective was compromised.

How did these dynamics affect her in the present? Although a very competent attorney, Marie was plagued with self-doubt. Of course, attorneys often find themselves in tense situations where emotions run high. Her choice of profession was a bit curious because of her inhibition about conflict but Marie solved this apparent contradiction by taking on research projects rather than litigation. She could gain some release from her competitive and aggressive surges by avoiding direct confrontation and vicariously enjoying her colleagues' legal maneuvering.

Interpersonally Marie was overly concerned of others' feelings toward her. She was able to make some nice friends who were very supportive but she became very anxious if anyone was angry with her, not truly able to trust in the genuine caring that her friends had demonstrated. Marie evaluated herself harshly and couldn't imagine that others didn't do the same.

Yet, Marie was no shrinking flower in all situations. Remember her unyielding demand for six children. With Luke she could be beyond assertive in her wishes, "steamrolling" him to submit. Her "working model" of conflict consisted of the dynamic of dominate or submit, with little in-between. Too much aggression infused her sexual relations as well. Her husband's desire for sexual contact became a demand for performance, in her mind an act of dominance and submission. Angry over being "dominated" Marie could not relax enough to "surrender" to her own sexual desire. Shame over sexual desires was prevalent, with the result of her either feeling bad for wanting to have sex, and bad for not.

All of this contributed to Marie often feeling, "in over her head" in life. Lacking confidence in her ability to negotiate situations with a modicum of aggression or conflict left her feeling perilously overmatched, often leading toward a regression into the dichotomy of dominance or submission. Although very effective in completing tasks either in work or at home, she felt ineffective in interpersonal arenas where contentiousness could arise.

By now we know enough from Marie's history to point out the determinants of her difficulties. Her overly aggressive and unattuned parents did not provide her with the tools to be and to feel effective in emotionally charged situations. Too much aggression and too much parental shaming were disabling.

Now to the other side: More effective parenting helps create a person who is, in turn, effective in navigating the hazards of life.

Louise, age forty-three, came for therapy after experiencing intense and unremitting grief after the death of her mother. Unquestionably the relationship with her mother had been difficult and had effects on her mental health and on her parenting but admirably she was able to put aside (to the extent possible) many of the noxious effects of her upbringing when raising her two boys. I say to the extent possible because a person can consciously attempt to mitigate the influences of family pathology but unconscious pressures will still exert an influence. Louise and I focused in our work together on helping her to not repeat with her children what she had experienced growing up. Providentially, Louise's husband Joe did not come with the same kind of emotional baggage that she did, and he was able to temper some of her occasional emotional missteps. In listening to Louise describe her sons, Sam and Mike, ages fourteen and sixteen, it seemed to me that they were quite healthy and well adjusted. I could tell, as could her boys, that she was immensely proud and delighted with them. But more importantly, they were proud of themselves, and felt that their accomplishments (academically and athletically) were due to their own talent and diligence and "belonged" to them and not to their parents. Their parents encouraged freedom of thought and expression and conveyed appreciation for the boys' ability to think on their own and to have opinions that might diverge from theirs. I was aware that they had the usual anxieties of children of those ages, but discerned little or no evidence of senses of shame or of out-of-the-ordinary inhibition. Since the parents did not externalize their aggression, the boys did not feel undone by conflict. Rather, each felt able to use his mind to solve conflicts without either excessive anger or shame.

We have seen two different child-raising paradigms with two vastly different outcomes. Now let's look at other scenarios that affect one's ability to confront conflict.

Curiosity vs. Criticism

As I will discuss in later chapters, educating patients, not just understanding the nature of the process of therapy but also illustrating to them the roots of their issues are crucial aspects of therapy. Earlier I spoke to this educative issue in regards to "upstairs" and "downstairs" aspects of the mind.

A not uncommon problem both within one's mind and within the therapeutic process is seen where individuals are more *critical* of their behavior, thoughts or feelings than *curious* as to the nature of their origins. In my work I emphasize (educate) that it is desirable both within one's mind and within therapy to be curious rather than critical. This is not to say that I think it is desirable to not feel self-critical at times. We all behave badly at times and we cannot exempt ourselves from careful self-scrutiny and to accept responsibility for our actions. But this is far different than intense and unending self-blame.

Individuals are often not aware that they are unduly critical. They may initially think that self-criticism is "normal" or deserved but I try to help them see that being highly self-critical is self-defeating and is a defense against openness of mind. As part of the educative process, I explain to those who have difficulty in describing activities of their life or of their mind in a reasonably noncritical fashion that it would be most helpful for them to "observe and report"; observe themselves and the workings of their mind, to note these activities and to report them to me at the next session. We can then examine these occurrences in an atmosphere of openness and curiosity.

I point to parental internalizations as a major causative factor in the tilting toward criticism and this intellectual knowledge helps the individual gain some distance from the heretofore sense of the inevitability of their ways of being. Eventually we will look more closely at the patient's conscious and unconscious fantasies and beliefs that contribute to their present-day owned sense of shame and guilt that elicits excessive criticism, but that process emerges after the patient has a firm understanding of his personality formation vis-à-vis parental influences.

Patients like Len whose ability to mentalize have been harmed by trauma tend toward the self-critical, sometimes violently so. Having incorporated parental identifications that externalized rather than thoughtfully handle conflict, Len had no model of careful consideration of the meanings of his or other actions. Rather he acted impulsively, sometimes becoming too angry and confrontational, or alternatively strongly self-blaming. Both of these options foreclose any exploration of what lay underneath his emotional outburst. In fact Len favored impulsivity since it afforded him an opportunity to "discharge" affects, protecting himself from the awareness of the emotional pain that fueled the outbursts. In this sense, the criticism (directed either externally or internally) operates both as affect management and as defense. Defense, as I mentioned, since the blaming took up so much mental space, there was no possibility of him delving into painful feelings and memories, or even of further elaboration of his thought processes.

His tendency toward blame also developed from a deficiency in his mental functioning, as his internal world was a legacy from identifications with parents who had similar predilections. The degree of symptomology is in direct relation to the degree of original pain. In this case, Len's morbid obesity and thought-numbing psyche, confirmed by his history, are indicative of severe early trauma.

Because of the far-reaching effects of trauma, helping him open up his mind to more thoughtful consideration and curiosity required a lot of work, both educative and therapeutic. I felt that it was important to help Len intellectually grasp the importance of curiosity in order to at least set up a touchstone for him to return to for when we therapeutically delve more deeply into painful affects and memories. I will save further discussion on how Len and I accomplished this task for later.

Shame and Guilt—Affects of Misdeeds

Patients are often imprecise in describing their dysphoria. Many know that they are unhappy but have trouble finding words to convey their subjective experience. For example, individuals may indicate that they are depressed when in actuality it is not so clear what "being depressed" feels like. For some it is sadness, for others lethargy and fatigue, or perhaps a sense of anxious foreboding. This same imprecision occurs with guilt and shame. The words "guilt" or "shame" are summary words that collapse into one syllable a complicated array of conscious and unconscious emotions and their underpinnings.

At times it is only under careful questioning and observation by the astute therapist that it can be determined whether the patient is feeling guilt, shame, both or neither. And even more importantly it is crucial to elaborate the intimate thoughts, feelings, associations, and memories that are called forth when one feels guilt and/or shame. Guilt is a statement that one has done (or always does) something (or some things) wrong or incorrect. Shame is the message that one is, at the moment at least, wrong to the core. It is unwise to say that one is more painful than the other but I would certainly say that shame is more impervious to therapeutic effect, since shame seems to develop earlier in the child's life and may feel to be more of the bedrock of the individual's internal makeup. I also think that most people would rather feel that they've done something wrong as opposed to feeling that their very essence is flawed. The former holds more hope for redemption.

Does it make any difference whether we correctly identify the dysphoria as being related to either guilt or shame? Mostly yes, and a little bit no. In therapy it is essential that the problematic affect is not only identified but is "felt" in the process. It is this "felt" experience and the consequent deconstruction of the guilt or shame dynamic between patient and therapist that is curative. If the proper distinction between shame and guilt is not made, the patient loses out on recapturing and reexperiencing defended-against affects and associations, not allowing a resolution of underlying issues. On the other hand, the in-the-moment work of the therapy is similar regardless of whether the patient struggles with shame or guilt. The patient's associations within the context of the understood character structure guide the therapist, and the therapist's interpretation will emphasize guilt or shame, depending on the nature of the matter at hand, but the process of listening, exploring, empathy and interpretation is quite similar regardless of the underlying issues.

Shame and guilt are experienced in all three memory systems. An individual struggling with shame and/or guilt has discrete memories of times of guilt or shame, has an overall guilt-based or shame-based implicit level of organization, and the person has memories of the atmosphere of guilt or shame in the household of her youth. Guilt and shame dynamics are pervasive and can be available verbally at times, but often exist in preconscious and unconscious venues.

In Marie's situation, the nature of her self-judging derived from her early internalized object relations. And this is the same for everyone. Often people will be bewildered by their inability to shake off anxiety, guilt or shame, believing that it "makes no sense" for them to feel so awful. But they disregard the intense influence of their internal world, over so-called reality. I often tell patients that psychic reality trumps external reality, hands down. The agony of these feelings can be close to intolerable and can result in many maneuvers designed to minimize them—substance abuse, eating disorders, dissociation—to name a few. Psychotherapy that is designed to look at both "upstairs" and "downstairs" dimensions can have a gradual mitigating effect and bring great relief, once one understands the "irrational" reasons for the distress.

But now let's explore each affect in more detail.

Shame

Erik Erikson (1950) elucidated various developmental stages. He labeled the second, corresponding to the child's second and third years of life as the period of "autonomy vs. shame or doubt." Although I am sure that Erikson is correct regarding the major developmental challenge at that particular age, I do believe that various pressures *throughout* the young child's life contribute to a sense of autonomy and self-confidence on the positive side, and shame and/or doubt on the negative. What is meant by *autonomy*? An individual who is autonomous can make decisions that serve to enhance his best interests without feeling undone by the influences of significant others in his orbit. Autonomy also means being reasonably free from pressures to conform to expectations derived from internalization of parental expectations. I am not suggesting that one should be so self-absorbed or oblivious that others' opinions don't count but that, in the best situation, one gathers important information from others but makes his own decision without being overly concerned with others' feelings or beliefs.

Many writers (Miller, 1996; Morrison, 1989) have highlighted the pervasive, pernicious and debilitating effects of shame. Shengold (1978) chillingly describes "soul murder," which "refers to killing the joy in life and interfering with the sense of identity of another human being. It is primarily a crime committed against children" (457). One effect of this kind of trauma is for the child to respond to problematic and conflictual situations with intense feelings of shame. Kohut (1971) indicated that shame is the inevitable consequence of one raised in an environment where the child's normal narcissistic needs are trampled. Although it is clear to me that shame is not only a consequence of trauma but is a ubiquitous human experience, I will concentrate on those whose level of shame is beyond the usual.

Typically too much shame results from parents who react, strongly or consistently, with a sense of disgust and disapproval to their child's feelings, thoughts or behavior. As Erikson (1950) states; "Shame supposes that one is completely exposed and conscious of being looked at: in one word, self-conscious" (252). He goes on to describe two constellations: Either the individual, in order to avoid a feeling of shame, obliterates the self, making one "invisible" to "shaming eyes" or "obliterates" others making their "shaming eyes" "invisible." In both cases the person in question is ruthless in the process of the denial of self and others' desires, in order to protect from the possibility of shame. Erikson goes on: "Doubt is the brother of shame" (Erikson, 1950, 253), as a shame-based individual cannot feel free to make decisions as every action is subject to the possibility of humiliation. Concern over others' judgment makes one not sufficiently autonomous. Conflict is untenable as one is frozen by inhibition of thought, behavior or affect. This is seen quite clearly in Marie's case.

Guilt

Those who suffer from exaggerated senses of wrongdoing do not decry their essence; rather they castigate themselves for their specific thoughts, feelings and actions. I am always intrigued when patients tell me they feel "guilty." I wonder exactly what they mean—Do they mean that they feel remorse—a profound sense of regret for their actions? Or do they feel anxiety that they might feel "bad" from their misconduct and if outed even worse from the opinions of others? Or, do they actually feel neither, but think that they "should" feel guilty when speaking about wrongdoings that others might find reprehensible? Even more confusing—if the individual disavows a sense of remorse for some activity "upstairs," are there "downstairs" uncomfortable feelings hidden from the supposed misbehaver?

What are the frightful consequences when guilt raises its ugly head? Freud pointed to three possibilities: loss of love, loss of object, and loss of relationships. By this he means that the guilty party may lose a sense of being loved if the misbehavior is discovered, or a loss of the loved one (loved one withdraws) or that the relationship ends permanently. The individual also can fear the loss of his own sense of well being as when his misbehavior turns his positive internal objects into negative ones, the result being that he becomes self-attacking (the self-object internalized relationship becomes infused with anger and guilt).

As I mentioned earlier, psychic reality outweighs so-called objective reality such that one can find himself in the throes of anxiety and guilt despite reassurances from the person who he feels he has wronged, as the guilty party might feel he has violated some sanction derived from childhood. Or the present-day (upstairs) "crime" evokes feelings from the past (downstairs). Further, in terms of remorse, the person may violate his own sense of right or wrong, and negative affect results from that loss of love, in this case self-love.

Case Example

I am going to describe a case of therapy with a patient whose unfortunate personality package contained copious amounts of both guilt and shame. James (mentioned in chapter 3) and his wife originally came to see me in the midst of severe marital discord. It quickly became clear that the marriage was doomed as neither partner really seemed to love the other, having married for a number of not very sound reasons. Despite the lukewarm temperature of their love, emotions run hot in most marital treatments, and they did here as well. As feelings intensified in the therapy, James became more and more distraught, but not over potential feelings of loss or sadness should his marriage end. Rather, he became increasingly anxious and eventually developed an intense germ phobia and compensatory hand-washing compulsion. Understanding and accepting the inevitable, his wife found her way out of both the marriage and the therapy while James fortunately continued in treatment.

How can we understand these twists and turns? Together, James and I traced his compulsion to an attempt to be cleansed of a sense of "badness" that derived, in adult experience, from a premarital sexual experience of some years past. Sometime after the affair, the woman informed him that she was concerned that she might have some sort of sexually transmitted disease. Despite the eventual knowledge that neither had any STD, he became concerned that he might still be in danger, certainly from his past involvement but also from any future contacts. Once married his fear receded quite a bit. As his marriage faltered, his anxiety increased correspondingly. James became intensely anxious about germs and disease, washing a number of times a day, panicking over any even far-fetched notion of "contamination" by what may have scarcely looked like blood or mucus and then avoiding any new relationships fearful of catching some dread disease. What triggered his intense symptom development? It was our sense that his "mistake" in marrying his wife (for intense sexual reasons) matched what he felt had been a horrific mistake in becoming sexually involved with a "dangerous" woman in the past. This contemporary *shame* of his error in judgment felt the same as the *shame* he felt in his sexual desires. These two mistakes made him feel that he was frightfully and shamefully out of control. Guilt and shame were also quite intertwined. As an adolescent he was "caught" in a sexual relationship with a girl who was considered to be the neighborhood "tramp." His father castigated him, "Can't you keep it in your pants?" in a shame-inducing fashion. His mother expressed disappointment for his behavior as well, creating intense feelings of guilt for his sexual desires.

I pointed out to him that his adolescent sexual behavior might not have been wise, but it wasn't out of range for a boy of his age, trying to help him see that shame or guilt are not givens in these sexual forays. Nevertheless, his internal objects held tight, and guilt and shame were unending. Further, James's mother was apparently a very attractive woman, and James had vaguely disturbing memories of amorous desires toward her in childhood and was filled with anxiety should anyone know about it—either his mother from whom he might feel like a dirty, bad boy, or from his father, whose wrath and disapproval he feared. All in all James felt attracted to women but also viewed them as present-day excitations of past forbidden desires. His anxiety over what his family perceived as shameful behavior helped to create his obsessive-compulsion character, of which doubt and indecision predominate.

James had two problematic senses of self—either he was a "bad boy" (guilt) or a "dirty boy" (shame) and these two negative self-images would inflame his anxiety like wildfire. Remember what Erikson said about "damning eyes"? James tried to hide himself from view of others through both OCD rituals and cryptic communication (I had a lot of trouble understanding him because of his elliptical allusions to matters of concern, rather than straightforward descriptions). Others' needs he would disavow as a way of minimizing their importance to him—he made them invisibly unimportant.

I've never had a therapeutic case that wasn't frustrating—it is the nature of the beast—and this case wasn't the most frustrating but did have its moments. The cause for this was that James doubted not only his ideas and desires, but mine as well. There were two main reasons for this. First, as a result of his wish to keep me invisible and unimportant (not able to make him feel guilty or ashamed) and second because of his desire to make me impotent, as if my potency would limit his. In his mind he was still that little boy who knew nothing who had transgressed into the world of adult sexuality.

Conflict needed to be avoided for fear that he might need to proclaim either desire or point of view. Either of which would open him to the possibilities of feeling crushing feelings of guilt or intense sense of mortification. His elliptical verbalizations puzzled others and limited intense conversations. He was also very much of a gamesman, calculating his interactions with others to maximize benefit and to minimize loss and humiliation. Although this might be a good strategy in poker (of which he was an aficionado), others, including me, did not feel that he was being open and honest, and this limited both intimate relationships and his ability to interact with others profitably during conflict.

James and I are making headway but with many stops and starts. My approach has been to be quite patient, to inform him when I see him maneuvering to avoid intimacy with me, and to wait until he feels sufficiently safe in order to be able to engage with me, in order eventually to touch upon his mortifying internal feelings of guilt and shame, engendered by desires denied.

The Nature of Attachments

Attachment, Individuation, and Separation

The need for human connectedness is inborn and essential and it is this necessity and complexity that provide ample opportunity for a multiplicity of problems to arise. A preeminent scholar in early attachment theory

(Bowlby, 1969) indicates that the quality of childhood attachment will affect later ability to establish and maintain relationships, and difficulties in early attachment are linked to multiple adult psychological dysfunctions. I don't think that anyone would question these assertions. Fortunately, the psychotherapeutic endeavor is a relationship—a place of attachment and its vicissitudes, providing an excellent venue for these issues to find expression, and then illuminating a path toward resolution

As might be expected, parental difficulties in these areas are likely to be nonconsciously passed on to their children. Parents may fervently wish to not burden their offspring with their own anxieties but the old adage, "Do what I say, not what I do" works as poorly here as anywhere else. Powerful needs like those of attachment, both healthy and not, often find fertile ground for growth in the parent-child relationship. In other words, the parents' internal objects and relationships become externalized onto the child, which she then internalizes (combined with other factors such as experience and temperament). Also, of course there are often two parents with two internal worlds, which in turn creates a fascinating and complicating internal mixture. This amalgam is what I have earlier referred to as the implicit level of personality functioning. Bowlby uses the term "internal working model" in similar fashion.

Most attachment theorists (Ainsworth et al., 1978; Main and Solomon, 1986; Blatt, 2006, to name a few) speak of individuals being either securely or insecurely attached. Within the insecure attachment category, Blatt (2006) postulates two different styles:

> Resistant attachment involves an intense preoccupation with maintaining contact with the need-gratifying figure and is accompanied by considerable anxiety in response to separation and loss. Avoidant attachment involves intense efforts at maintaining an aloofness and detachment to deal with loss; these efforts are defensive expressions of exaggerated autonomy and independence to deal with loss. (108)

Blatt goes on to connect resistant attachment with the development of higher than usual dependent needs, while avoidant attachment is seen in those who tend to be more isolative and internally focused. While I don't doubt that individuals can be broadly placed in such categories, I believe that such categorization can run the risk of simplifying extremely complex dynamics, that exist at varying levels of consciousness, and that become activated differently depending on the stimulus of a given situation. In developing what I feel is a more comprehensive picture of attachment and personality, Wallin (2007) points out that internal working models, attachment styles and reflective function all contribute to a picture of one's general level of attachment, to what can be considered attachment health.

What about separation and individuation? Although a developmental goal is for a child to be able to gradually navigate the world on his own, it is also hoped that sound early attachment not only allows the child to "lean" on his healthy internal objects, but to be able to find healthy external objects to lean on throughout his life. So a healthy separation and individuation process is first of all gradual, and secondly, always retains remnants of early life, both as sustenance and as paradigms of relationships. Separation is relative, and healthy separation and individuation leads toward healthy autonomy and healthy later relationships.

Rachel is one whose attachment anxieties stood out loud and clear. Rachel lost her mother to leukemia at age fifteen. Her father shows little in the way of intensity of attachment, as evidenced by his infrequent visits to her, his rather feeble attempts to connect with her, his hypercriticalness and his discomfort when she is distressed. Rachel has never married, instead was involved with a man of differing religious background who never showed much inclination to either marry her or to form the kind of union we hope to see in committed relationships. After seventeen years of increasing despair over the staleness of their relationship, Rachel finally consulted me for assistance. Initially I met with her and her boyfriend Tom, but her individual need for therapy took precedence over other treatment options. Fortunately the boyfriend had a therapist of his own. At a later point, I referred them to a couples therapist to assist them.

It didn't take long in our therapy for it to become apparent that Rachel was dreadfully unhappy, certainly about the relationship, but more importantly and poignantly over the sense of emptiness in her life. To compensate, Rachel was physically and socially active to the extreme, spending much of her spare time exercising, dancing, and taking a variety of other classes, all of which, on the surface, were beneficial but also were expressions of her need to keep herself so busy that she couldn't think about her despair.

During our brief conjoint therapy Tom would "accuse" her of having "an attachment disorder." Of course "accusing" one is neither endearing nor palatable, and although Rachel herself acknowledged some truth in his forays into diagnosis, she understandably felt defensive. Very little is solely circumstance in the world of the psyche, and the fact that Rachel would choose, let alone stay with someone like Tom, who was both nonempathic and critical, fit her internal objects, derived from her uninvolved and oft times unsympathetic parents and from their own relationship which appeared, as near as I could tell, to be rather listless. Regardless of Tom's accuracy in his conceptions of Rachel's problems, he had plenty of commitment issues of his own. Not surprisingly, the treatment with Tom went nowhere fast and she eventually left the relationship but with some bouts of panic and anxiety. In these times, she tearfully lamented that she was afraid, "that I would have no one to take care of me."

Rachel and Tom were perfect foils for each other. Neither really felt comfortable with a close relationship, and their attachment to each other was full of fondness but lacked intensity and intimacy. I felt that Rachel, and Tom from my more distant sense of him, were still attached to their unavailable, in Rachel's case, and overwhelming, in Tom's case, mothers. Tom needed to maintain distance in order to maintain a sense of separateness and individuality; he feared suffocation. Rachel was afraid of the experience of intense yearning and rejection. Each pushed and pulled, trying to get close but not too close. Conflicts that involve attachment concerns often have this push-pull quality.

Let's apply our conceptions about attachment to Rachel and her relationships. From outward appearances, Rachel's attachment could be considered mostly avoidant. As I mentioned, the complexity of the mind is not and should not be easily reduced to categories. So, although she might be avoidant of relationships, she avoids for a good reason, to protect from reexperiencing profound feelings of loss that originated in childhood. In other words, if we establish that the need for attachment is inborn, then we must recognize that this need does not disappear; rather it is defensively supplanted by avoidant and resistant attachment patterns. As we can see, Rachel's attachment concerns are neither fish nor fowl; on the surface she seems quite disinterested in attachment, yet she has remained involved with Tom for seventeen years, about sixteen of them unhappy. Further, her panic when the relationship dissolves indicates a very strong attachment; even it is more about security than love. Soon after she left Tom she became involved with another man, and after him, another. I told her that she reminded me of a trapeze artist, not willing to let go unless she had someone else holding his hand out to her. Rachel's level of "attachment health" is determined by her past attachment pleasures and disappointments and by her ability or lack to reflect upon such matters.

Psychotherapy as relationship is the perfect vehicle for attachment matters to emerge, and a felicitous venue for resolution to occur. For Rachel and me this means we often focus on a discussion of her feelings about me, and to some extent my feelings about her. In doing so Rachel gains more mentalizing and reflective ability, has more of a sense of her "downstairs" containing conflicts, begins to feel safer and less vulnerable, all of which in turn will have an effect on her outside relationships.

How does secure and insecure attachment impact upon conflict resolution? Let's turn to a discussion on affect management for perspective on this.

Affect Management

Affects or emotions are the fuel that powers the machinery of the psyche. They are the glue that holds relationships together. How one handles "wants" help determine whether conflict is unmanageable or is processed relatively comfortably.

In the previous chapter I wrote about affect management from the perspective of "open" and "closed minds." Affect management can also be considered from the point of view of self and other regulation. Beebe and Lachmann (2005) point out that attachment paradigms from childhood set down patterns of experience, which determine how the individual learns to meet and regulate her own affects, how she will imagine others will respond to her affects, and how she will respond to the affects of others. These are patterns of self and mutual affect regulation, a part of character structure.

Let's look at Len's affective and relationship expectations. Because of Len's family experiences he anticipates that he will not be heard if he makes a reasonable complaint to his wife; instead he expects indifference. Consequently in a tense situation, he silently attempts to handle his frustration internally and single-handedly. Eventually frustration gets the best of him, and he angrily explodes. At this point, his wife (with her own internal representations), his chosen and willing partner in this drama, becomes reassuring and apologetic for her perceived misdeed, and relationship calm is reestablished, but with little in the way of illuminating discourse. This is no different than what would occur in childhood, both between him and his parents and between his parents. Needs were not routinely responded to unless they became highly intense. The affective glue of attachment alternated between indifference, explosiveness and reassurance.

Len's ability to process affects was compromised by the deficits in his early relationship patterns, one major explanation for his need to nurture himself through copious amounts of food. Many others turn to outside sources (drugs, alcohol, etc.) as attempts to salve their inner distress. Or they may create interpersonal dramas as Len does where he discharges emotion, then regains his emotional equilibrium, and finally cements his bond with his wife who was prone to drift off into her own internal world of self and other neglect.

As painful as this dynamic is, it is still felt to be better than the abject aloneness each fears.

Attachment health is one aspect of the internal representation; ego strength is another. The ego operates, in the best of circumstances, to maximize an individual's pleasure and satisfaction, and to minimize discomfort. Of course we are well aware that this paradigm does not always work as well as we would like. When it doesn't we have psychological disorder, the severity depending, in part, on the degree of ego dysfunction. The ego also processes affects, and its structural capability determines whether stimulating experiences are handled with ease or are so intense that symptoms develop.

Secure attachment experiences contribute greatly to ego strength. The individual internalizes positive relationship experiences that become an internal template of expectations within life, resulting in healthy methods of affect regulation. Experiences with parents who are securely attached create the internal mind set that challenges can be met with success as the individual has not only the intrinsic belief in himself but also has the actual talent to problem solve without undue distress.

The healthy individual "leans" upon his healthy internalized objects for reassurance and sustenance. Stimulating events that may trouble those who do not have healthy internalized representations are met with relative equanimity with those with healthier representations. For example, Rachel became panicky initially when she separated from Tom, even though the relationship was not the best. But with a paucity of nurturing internal objects to rest upon, Rachel was left feeling adrift and without foundation. In many ways Rachel is quite capable, but her attachment history created some fissures in her ego structure, preventing her from being able to weather the intense emotions engendered by separation. If one cannot feel a sense of security, one has difficulty in enduring conflict, and is likely to avoid or feel overwhelmed by tension either internally or externally in relationships.

Discharge versus Healthy Expression of Affects

Joyce would often say to me, "What am I supposed to do with my feelings? I want to get rid of them, I feel like I'm going to explode." This is what I refer to as a *discharge problem*, such that Joyce lacks the more adaptive problem-solving skills of mentalizing and self-reflection that would enable her to process affects more comfortably. We can turn to her parent-child experiences to understand her difficulties. Her mother's overcontrolling nature suggests that the mother, too, was afraid of emotion. She was also prone to emotional outbursts, not providing Joyce with a positive model of affect management.

When Joyce was "naughty" mother would move away from her sadistically, refusing to speak or comfort her. Consequently Joyce's sense of attachment was tenuous, such that separation meant abandonment and loss of love. Joyce internalized these representations and could not generate positive reassuring affect when upset. Instead she desired to expel her feelings, hoping to gain satisfaction from the expulsion just as mother sadistically expelled her affects. It is notable that her mother was famous for her love of enemas for her children, again setting up the expectations that internal activities could not be regulated naturally but required outside interference.

Because of the tension that became activated in conflict-laden situations, Joyce finds talking therapy difficult. She wants action, not talk. She wants me to be like her mother, and instruct her how to feel better. My therapeutic plan was to empathize with her discomfort to the extent I could (to help create a more benign self-other internalized representation), to model reflection and mentalizing and to encourage the same from her, and to help her to identify the hidden intense sadness that she felt over the traumas of her life. Very, very gradually, Joyce became able to process her affects with more thoughtfulness and less explosiveness.

Anger vs. Hostility

Luke and Marie would often end up verbally hurting each other when they had marital squabbles. They had no internal conception that one could be angry without being hostile. In fact this is not an uncommon occurrence for many whose experiences within the family reinforced the confusion between anger and hostility. Those who find hostility appealing are embroiled in a sadomasochistic dynamic such that they can't imagine that someone is not trying to hurt them during angry interchanges. Anger is not a particularly pleasant emotion, and although an angry person is trying to forcefully communicate that something is amiss in an interpersonal experience, it does not always hold that the angry person is hostile, trying to gain pleasure from another's pain.

Those prone to the "paranoid position" often find partners who are similarly positioned such that conflicts are often dealt with through aggressive outbursts. It is important to remember that this anger-hostility dimension is not solely the province of interpersonal relations. Luke and Marie were not only hostile to each other, they were hurtful and unforgiving within their own internal world.

Any psychic enterprise can be a defense against another and this premise holds true in this arena. Luke and Marie would rather be hostile than vulnerable, angry instead of sad, verbally aggressive instead of afraid, and stubborn instead of "weak." An important aspect of psychotherapy is to identify the defenses in order to enable the patient to be in touch with these more tender feelings. In doing this, the individual has more access to a multiplicity of feeling states, creating more complexity within relationships. Since Luke and Marie each feared their vulnerable sides, they had a vested interest in keeping themselves at odds. Our therapy was designed to help them work through this dynamic in order that they could feel safe with each other and then more intimate.

Intrapsychic Conflict

Intrapsychic conflict is ubiquitous, and the ample psychotherapeutic literature reflects this. The subject is too complex to even attempt to do justice to a full discussion. Intrapsychic means conflicts between competing aspects of the psyche. Although I have not labeled the conflicts that I have described already as being "intrapsychic," most of them are. But since the term "intrapsychic" is one commonly discussed, I feel it is important to at least specify its nature and its components, and I will do so here and in the following chapter on defenses.

All of us wish to be in balance psychically. However, one's mind is not always so cooperative. Competing desires, ambiguities, ambivalences, conflicts between wishes and self-criticism, etc., all point out how the mind is never at rest but is always complicated and dynamic.

As I have indicated earlier, a symptom is an attempt to make the best of a bad situation. I have just described how Luke and Marie, despite loving each other and wanting a closer relationship, "choose" to maintain distance despite their desires. Each was internally conflicted (manifested externally as well) in that the fear of vulnerability conflicted with the desire for closeness. Each developed a compromise—close but not too close. Psychotherapy is designed to identify these internal conflicts, to help the individual to understand the workings of their minds (defenses) and to then access the affect (in Luke and Marie's cases vulnerability) that then allows the freedom to be closer and more tender with each other (and with themselves). This has generative effect, freeing each in other areas of life and psyche.

Desire

It may be easier to thread a needle with a camel than to discuss in brief matters of desire, and of sexual desire in particular. But I will try to illuminate

some salient matters as to how desire is not only central to healthy functioning but can be a source of considerable intrapsychic conflict.

If affects are the fuel for the psyche, desire is its octane. Intensity of emotions is at base, a favorable quality. Liveliness, enthusiasm, zest for life, a healthy appetite, strong sexual desire, hopes for success and achievement, needs for relatedness, etc., are all affects that we find worthwhile. Unfortunately, those who have had experiences that were too stimulating find affect management difficult, and rather than desires being pleasurable, they become problematic.

When patients come in for treatment they often feel blocked in their emotional life—deadened, depressed, listless and anxious. These states represent certain bodily experienced states. Young children are supremely focused on their bodies and sensations, and these in-the-body states are the progenitors of later affects and desires. If these desires are dealt with by shame, derision or disapproval, the natural level of bodily excitement becomes stultified and inhibited. In some cases, desires become overmanaged resulting in inhibition (sexual desire as an example); with others desires are "undermanaged" and are expressed without due consideration and explosively. The quality of the underlying ego structure and the strength of healthy attachments and internalizations will determine how desires are acted upon—whether the individual can find ways for comfortable gratification, or if the individual feels overcome by overstimulation. A major goal of therapy is to assist the patient to explore his anxiety about affect in order to find new and more satisfying ways of emotional expression, finding the grace to be neither out of control nor overcontrolled.

Sexual Desire

Every patient who graces a therapist's consulting room does so because some aspect of psychological functioning is impeded. The compromise formations that were developed in childhood are not as successful as one would hope and are allowing too much anxiety, depression, maladaptive behavior or other symptoms to emerge. This is probably no clearer than in the realm of sexual desire. And general interest in sexuality is certainly obvious in the avalanche of publications and discourses. As we know that no aspect of the psyche exists independent of any other, we see that sexuality is impacted by multiple sources, both conscious and unconscious. So, for instance, attachment issues will impact sexual desire and activity, concerns about power and efficacy will as well, the freedom or lack thereof of emotional expression will enhance or limit sexuality, self-esteem will have a major effect, conflicts over aggression will derail comfort in sexual activity, inhibitions about pleasure will obviously have a huge impact, and so on. The statement that sexual desire is often associated with intense feelings of shame and/or guilt will surprise no one. Not only that but the strength of sexual desire is like a siren call for many psychological issues to find their expression. In other words, all of the attributes and experiences that make up character structure will impact the degree of satisfaction one is able to achieve sexually.

It is always fascinating how people "find" each other in a fashion that matches their internal objects and relationships, and sexuality is not immune from this attempt to find contemporary solutions for past frustrations. The conflicts within become the conflicts outside.

Luke and Marie's relationship has been strongly affected by fears of condemnation and humiliation, and about issues of power and attachment. Luke has strong sexual desires toward his wife; when rebuffed he becomes furious, feeling disrespected. This feeds into his barely dormant sense of being a failure as a potent man, valued solely as a progenitor, not as a lover. Marie finds sexual desire to be overwhelming, afraid of her intensity of affect, fearful of the outward expression of her needs, dreading vulnerability and shame, all the time questioning Luke's motives. Luke and Marie each approach their sexuality from their internalized representations, their fantasies and beliefs about themselves as sexual beings, their individual histories, sexual and otherwise, their conceptions of gender and gender roles, their ability to permit hedonic pleasure, their comfort with intimacy, their trust with each other, their concerns with shame and/or guilt, their ability to allow aggression and sexual desire to complement each other, their sense of agency and integrity over their own bodies, their sense of themselves as sensual beings, and their ability to give over to their own and to their partner's desire. A complicated mix to be sure. No wonder so many struggle with comfortable satisfaction of sexual desire. Sexuality, being so central to the human condition, is not only rife for problems to emerge, but is also a potent venue for many psychic struggles to make themselves known, and to then become available for analysis and treatment.

The work of psychodynamic therapy is not to focus solely on symptomology but is to concentrate on the background causative factors with the expectation that this approach has both more wide-ranging and more lasting effects. This has been the case with Luke and Marie; the work consisting of deconstructing family dynamics and identifying and interpreting how these dynamics negatively impact their individual and relationship functioning, and the manner in which they manage excitement intrapsychically.

Concluding Thoughts

In this chapter I have continued my discussion on aspects of the psyche that impact on psychological functioning and on the ability to deal with conflict. The more that one delves into the psyche its complexity becomes obvious, with intricate and complex interactions. Most aspects of the psyche are multiply determined and layered through the different levels of consciousness. No wonder that intensive psychotherapy is most effective with frequent sessions over a period of some years.

Next I turn to methods of defense, with a longer discussion on dissociation, a protective mechanism that can be subtle yet devastating in its effects.

CHAPTER SIX

The Partitioned Mind

The ego has numerous functions. Its main job is as CEO of the psyche. The ego, in the best of circumstances, is designed to provide support to the individual, as one would do for an employee in a well-run company. To do this, it identifies internal needs and scans the environment to determine if these needs can be met safely. It has a synthetic function, bringing together disparate psychic aspects for adaptive purposes. It operates a person's defenses. The ego is neither static nor uniform. It must adjust to environmental and internal stimulation and figure out ways in which to satisfy competing desires. In doing so, we can consider the ego to, at times, be partitioned. In this chapter I investigate this partitioning of the psyche, representing methods of keeping one's sense of self intact, needs satisfied, guilt and shame minimized and affects tolerable.

In its business dealings the ego becomes partitioned, sometimes as defense, other times as self-states. In reference to defense, the ego splits *vertically*, an attempt to maintain two contradictory notions. For instance, Maggie will put out of her mind awareness that a given "friend" has acted unconscionably toward her, but can easily recognize the "reality" of the relationship with a small bit of prompting. Other times the ego splits *horizontally*, in keeping awareness of troubling feelings, thoughts and memories out of awareness. Differing self-states are also an indication of the partitioning of the ego.

Defenses

The tension between a patient's desire to resolve his psychological dysfunction and his wish to not deal with painful material creates a fascinating oscillation within the mind, and correspondingly in therapy, between revealing and concealing. The ego's defensive apparatus is designed to protect the individual from becoming overwhelmed by uncomfortable thoughts or feelings. Defenses are not the enemy; we all need defenses lest affects overwhelm and interfere with everyday life and activities. Yet, these defenses can work too well, preventing access to feeling states that enliven one's life, or not work well enough, in not performing the crucial task of affect management. In chapter 3 I described ways in which the therapist gains access to the patient's hidden internal world. I described various methods of defense and gave examples of the ways in which these defenses are worked with therapeutically. In the previous chapter, I introduced the notion of intrapsychic conflict. I will expand my discussion of defenses in this section, within the context of conflict.

Defenses operate to negate an aspect of experience. Repression (I don't remember), denial (it didn't happen), reaction formation (it's not bad, it's good), suppression (let's not talk about it), projection (it's not me, it's you) are all examples of the attempt to alter the reality of a given thought or feeling.

Conflict evokes defensive maneuvering. As I described in the second chapter, an individual develops nonconscious algorithms or expectations based upon past stimulus and responses as how to respond in emotionally laden situations. These expectations are subject to distortion via defense, as when "emotional forecasting" is based more on the past experiences than on a realistic appraisal of the present-day realities or future probabilities. Here are two examples: First, Sophie was worried about a medical problem that might be worsened by her psychotropic medications. After discussing with her psychiatrist the possibility of eliminating the medication, she raised the issue with me. I told her that I appreciated her concern about her health, hoped that we could discuss the pros and cons and suggested that we would be alert to consequences of the reduction in her medication, should she decide in that direction. In the next session she was very upset with me, wondering why I was not supportive of her decision to go off the meds. I was surprised by her reaction since I was certain that I did not react in the way she suggested. When queried further, Sophie also indicated that she felt that her psychiatrist was not going to be supportive of the decision to alter her medication regimen either. The gleam in her eye revealed to me that she was itching for a fight. How to make sense of this? Sophie was forecasting incorrectly that both the psychiatrist and I would be nonsupportive. But she was using her misperception of our reactions as a defense against *her* anticipated and feared reaction. Sophie is understandably very upset about the choice she has to make—either jeopardize her mental health of her physical well-being. She is all too familiar with the world of despair. On the other hand, she is no stranger to rage and blame, as they were familiar responses within the family and have now become defenses against more upsetting feelings. Being faced with a choice with two frightening alternatives (mental health vs. physical health problems) activates fears of despondency. In defense, Sophie "chooses" anger, by inaccurately forecasting both the psychiatrist's and my reaction.

Second example: Joe "says" to himself, "if John (or probably anyone significant to him) looks unhappy, I will withdraw because I am afraid of John's anger." This is not a conscious conversation but represents Joe's implicit idea of what he should do in situations of potential conflict. But besides understanding the nature of his pattern of conflict avoidance, the question remains to be asked, "what is so intolerable about anger?" In Joe's case he might have had childhood traumatic experiences where anger was out of control and he feels incapable of tolerating his and others' anger. Or, he might have unconscious feelings of guilt that might activate a feeling that he is being "found out" for his imagined or real unconscionable behavior. Or shame might be lurking, ready to be activated. Therapy is designed to not only help the patient to free up defended-against affects, but also to understand the workings of his mind. To this end, understanding the nature of one's defensive operations (Grey, 1994; Busch, 1995) is no less important than comprehending the hidden reasons for the defenses. The process of therapy, by my lights, is to get beyond the "fear of anger" and to explore the deeper layers of affects, fantasies and defenses that give rise to the conflict. The therapist's task is to assist the patient and his tender ego to feel safe enough to disclose painful secrets that he has kept, via defense, hidden. To do this it is essential that the patient feels understood and emotionally held, and not made to feel that he is purposefully hiding or "resisting" the therapist.

Defenses in Action

A therapist listens to the patient's associations with his trained ear searching for underlying concerns and conflicts, and for the defenses keeping these matters hidden. As I have indicated, intensity of affect is in general a positive quality; it is only when this intensity is derived from too much or too little childhood stimulation that it becomes problematic. Maggie struggles to maintain a sense of calm despite intense feelings. We know that as a child Maggie was flooded by emotions from the combination of too much stimulation and too little nurturance. She developed defensive strategies that were adaptive at the time of her traumas but now compromise her ability to find satisfaction and peace. Let's take a look at her defensive strategies, and how they can be addressed in therapy. Maggie, rather mainstream and conventional in lifestyle, told me that she had been invited to her hairdresser's sixtieth birthday party. Knowing from her previous description that he was a gay man who seemed to live on the outside edge of convention, I asked how she felt about the invitation. She said that she felt fine and was planning to attend. After the event, she told me she didn't know a soul and none of his other clients seemed to be there. The hairdresser and several of his friends were dressed in drag, and he put on a musical revue for the assemblage. "He doesn't look that great in makeup," she said rather sardonically. I asked her how she felt about being there. "I felt fine," she responded. My patient is very nonjudging and accepting of others but I still felt that the strangeness of the situation to her fairly conventional worldview would warrant some sort of emotional reaction. I noted this silently and listened to her further thoughts. She was unusually quiet, telling me that she just doesn't have much to say today. "Do you think that it has anything to do with your feelings about the party?" I wondered. She then became a bit anxious and more voluble. She now says that she realizes that she was uncomfortable but for some reason couldn't allow herself to know this. Maggie characteristically denies her feelings, as she is fearful that acknowledging any uncomfortable affects puts her at risk of feeling too much. This was adaptive to her as a child as no one was available or willing to help her with her strong feelings generated, in part by trauma, and now she ends up feeling estranged from her own feelings (as evidenced by the difficulty in associating and the absence of any feelings about the party). She disavows any affect in order to protect herself—to protect her from reexperiencing early "strange" occurrences of her early life when her father was sexually inappropriate, and when her mother beat her unmercifully, and other overstimulations. The cross-dressing was unexpected, again reminding her of unpleasant surprises of her youth. Once we discuss her defenses, the underlying distress emerges and she feels to be "more herself" again.

Maggie uses isolation (an idea removed of affect), denial (she didn't mind going), and disavowal (she didn't feel any affect). Larry, the compulsive hand washer, used obsessive-compulsive defenses against his sexual and attachment desires in order to feel clean and not dirty. Any psychic activity can be used as defense (Brenner, 1982). For instance, at times a patient will use the transference relationship to defend against awareness of past trauma. Or the patient might concentrate on past feelings in order to diminish feelings about the therapist in the present. Each person develops "favorite" defenses that serve to protect. These defenses can be conscious but many aspects are unconscious, including the conflicts activating them. As defense analysis progresses, the underlying concerns emerge and become less frightening and stultifying and conflict diminishes.

Enactments

Although I don't feel that I'm a mass of contradictions, I do act out of character occasionally, and the reasons for this are interesting and illuminating, and useful within life and within therapy. In the consulting room we refer to these as enactments, an intrusion into the self-state of psychotherapist by an urgency of affect or denial of such. For example, one time I indicated to Maggie that it was time for the session to stop; it was only after she left that I realized that I had let her go fifteen minutes early. Maggie returned to the next session, saying nothing about my gaffe. I raised it with her and she indicated that she didn't notice anything amiss. Now of course this defense is characteristic of Maggie who often doesn't want to see what is in front of her, an adaptive response from childhood (a "negative hallucination"). Well that explains Maggie's defense perhaps but does nothing to illuminate the reasons for me cutting the session short. Through my years of experience I have come to the realization that most enactments occur as a defense against the awareness of strong positive feelings. Upon reflection I came to the conclusion that this was the case here as well. As she and I discussed my error and her denial, I realized that both of us were uncomfortable with the intensity that we felt toward one another. Telling her this created some initial anxiety but was later helpful as we were able to discuss how denial of these feelings compromised our relationship in the therapy, and by extension (since we could not bring affects and defense available for analysis) made it difficult for her to establish strong relationships in her outside life.

Enactments represent important unconsciously generated conflicts that when addressed deepen and intensify the therapy. They develop in a way that is idiosyncratic to the couple and represent a creative enterprise where two personalities work together to bring out a matter that is beyond awareness. Although often initially uncomfortable, the exploration of these enactments (so long as they can be handled without either party becoming too hurtful) is always beneficial.

Self-States

We all act differently in different venues. I have a certain demeanor as a therapist, which is different than me as a husband, father or friend. These roles can be considered to be self-states. In a healthy personality, there is a coherence of attributes, through the different self-states, and the stability of the coherence is reassuring, particularly when tensions run high. As a therapist, for example, I can lean on my therapist identity when emotional intensity increases.

Although I never really lose my worldview as a psychotherapist, I need to leave it off to the side when I'm in engaged in other endeavors, like buying groceries on the weekend, but still need to have it at the ready on Monday morning. Some, though, find it to be quite difficult to move through different roles, their sense of stability threatened by the need to shift from one to another. For instance, Marie has difficulty in moving from the self-state of mother to that of sexual partner. Mother is a comfortable and reassuring role; sexual partner raises fears of intrusion and discomfort with her own sexual desires. Conflicts can easily emerge in the movement from one role to another, both within oneself and between others (as with Marie and Luke).

Self-states develop out of the child's need to develop a sense of differentiation between the "me" and the "not me." The child, through experience and feedback from significant people in her life, develops a way of thinking about herself: "I am someone who likes to play soccer, but I am not particularly fond of baseball." Or, "I am someone who feels energized by others, and I do not find solitary activity so pleasurable." These patterns of experience coalesce into states of being (self-states) that give order and definition to character structure. It is hoped that there is sufficient flexibility within these self-structures that they are available for revision as new information and experiences arise. In the healthy environment the child develops an organized sense of identity, with affects regulated by internalized attachment paradigms.

If early experiences are too jarring or parents are too controlling the child grows up not feeling ownership for her own choices and pleasures and feels threatened by others' intrusions. In these cases, stimuli from the environment can feel too stimulating, culminating in extreme anxiety and potential disruption to functioning (the ego is overwhelmed). Besieged by strange or novel situations, the ego is no longer coherent; instead it fragments into relatively disconnected self-states.

False, True and Empty Selves

In common circumstances, a person's sense of self varies throughout the day depending on external circumstances and internal mood states but still will feel connected to a vital and coherent inner self. But with those with traumatic backgrounds, the central ego, as Fairbairn (1952) points out, is quite weak and, instead, the psyche is dominated by unintegrated self-states that are not connected to an inner stable central self. In an attempt to forge a coherent identity, the patient urgently tries to keep these fragmented self-states together. But this generates an agglomeration of disparate selves, not an integrated self-organization. The creation of false selves is an effort to protect the fragile and treasured true or authentic self. As one patient put it, "I put up a wall to protect my heart."

Also, though, false selves are erected not only to protect the fragile "true self" but also to defend against the awareness of the "empty self." This empty state stands "behind," so to speak, the false self and operates as a strong motivator to keep the falseness front and center. The empty state is often a consequence of identification with absent, deadened parents. Internalizing absence creates a dark hole of nonexistence. This in turn creates a sense of abject aloneness and a desolate loss of hopefulness. It doesn't allow the flowering of emotional connectedness nor for the development of a full erotic and sensual life.

The possibility of experiencing emptiness is met with great horror and terror. When threatened by these feelings, panic reactions may ensue. Patients will often try a multitude of coping mechanisms to prevent experiencing profound despair, including calling upon the familiar but still reassuring sense of falseness and detachment. They live an "as-if" life. The empty self is not devoid of objects, it is only experienced as such, as self emptied of objects (Howard Erman, personal communication).

Working with patients with false or empty selves is no picnic. The therapy tends to be lifeless and deadening. The patient fears affects and because of this wants to deplete the therapy of any emotional vitality. Because of the lurking suicidal despair, each of the participants may unconsciously conspire to keep the therapy false, as falsity is still felt to be preferable to extreme despondency. The therapist, in order to be successful, must intellectually understand the life and death struggle and have the emotional fortitude to help each of them face what is felt to be nameless dread.

Dissociation

Dissociation, like the development of false and empty selves, can occur when stimulation is too intense and the ego splits and self-states become detached from the central ego. Dissociation is a defense but can also become a personality configuration, as in a Dissociative Personality, or even more severe,

Dissociated Identity Disorder (Multiple Personality). Dissociation is not just the province of the very disturbed; we all dissociate to some extent, in times of strong emotions, but it is very problematic for those whose coping skills are limited. Dissociation, like all defenses, comes about from conflict, but from conflict that feels too intense. It temporarily solves the problem of intensity by splitting off one part of the psyche from the other, but it is crippling since the individual does not have access to all of his faculties and is hobbled by the need to devote so much energy to keep feelings at such a remove. As Bromberg (2001) states,

> In other words, dissociation as a defense, even in a relatively normal personality structure, limits self-reflection to what is secure or needed for survival of selfhood, while in individuals for whom trauma has been severe, self-reflection is severely curtailed in order that the capacity to reflect does not break down completely and result in a collapse of self-hood. (12)

Conflict can be overwhelming when one lacks an ability to reflect upon oneself or on another's motives (mentalizing). A person with proclivities toward dissociation will have significant interpersonal problems since he or she will not be "all there" in relationships, especially when feelings heat up. This configuration can be puzzling and disquieting to others since it can be disorienting to be dealing comfortably with someone and then to find oneself embroiled in some sort of enactment, without warning or understanding.

The disparate self-states function to obliterate memory, substituting fogginess and confusion for intolerable psychic pain. Present-day conflicts are felt as no different from past traumas, resulting in affect storms and further withdrawal. These self-states are isolates and are burdened by conscious and unconscious sadomasochistic fantasies. Because of the chaos engendered, rapid shifts between self-states occur, as the person searches for safety, hoping to protect the fragile ego from too much aggression and fear. It's easy to see that interpersonal relationships are bound to suffer as conflicts between the self-states become externalized onto others. The recipient of the projection is bound to not be very pleased with the burden of negativity and is likely to push back aggressively.

I worked with Brad, age forty, who found himself frequently in conflict with his colleagues at his engineering firm, with others in his professional organization, and with some women at his place of employment who felt that he showed too much interest in their bodies. At other times, though, he was well liked and admired for his intelligence and capabilities. He was confused by his problems at work, not being able to have distance on his shifting moods, believing instead that others were overreacting.

As we deconstructed his story, we came to see that despite his obvious talents, he questioned his ability to function as a capable man and would "trip" into an aggressive and inappropriate self-state when he felt threatened. At work he had been struggling with completing an assignment and felt very badly about this, and he became self-attacking. I wondered with him on why we couldn't consider the reasons for his procrastination instead. Suddenly he turned on me and subjected me to a vicious diatribe that was stunning in its hurtful and sarcastic tone, pointing out that I had no right to speak with him of his inadequacies since I had little room to be "superior" as I had been two minutes late to starting the session. Although I intellectually understood what he was doing and what he felt he needed to do to me, I still felt threatened and angry and had brief fantasies of responding to him sarcastically. I didn't, and once I returned to my more normal level of equanimity he and I worked hard to understand what had transpired.

His history was of course highly significant. His father abused him emotionally and physically when he was a child. The verbal abuse included frequent allusions to him being less manly than his father, and that the sarcastic and sadistic implication that Brad was much more like his mother, in a "girly" sort of way. I asked him how he handled the barrage of insults and he told me that he would try to imagine that he was somewhere else. This was a dissociative response, and while he felt it was voluntary and conscious, it was also compellingly motivated by urgent nonconscious needs to protect his fragile sense of masculine potency. Along with this came compensatory sadomasochistic fantasies that he used in an attempt to maintain affect and release emotion without psychic implosion.

In our treatment, propelled by his difficulties at work, he dissociated from one self-state (interested and curious patient) into another (identified with the sadistic aggressor), when I tried to broach the subject of his procrastination. In "attacking the messenger" he projected his sense of inadequacy onto me (paranoid position). Provoked, I wanted to respond angrily, just as he had internally desired as a child. Not every therapist would have become enraged as I had. Clearly he touched on a sensitive spot of my own. Fortunately, though, I did not have the same need as he had to maintain a sadomasochistic dynamic. Through my own self exploration, and by pointing out the dynamic to Brad, I maintained the therapeutic relationship that allowed us to explore his typical (implicit) dissociative way of dealing with conflict, his need to punish himself (via putting himself in jeopardy at his job) for his aggression and his need to assert himself aggressively in order to counter a feared sense of masculine inadequacy. This process allowed him to then be more in touch with the underlying sadness and despair over his past treatment, and to help him to move on. This enactment, although difficult for both of us, ended well.

Concluding Thoughts

As with all other aspects of the psyche, the ego can be compromised by too much and too little; too much stimulation and too little internal sense of safety. Internal representations affect the ability of the ego to function effectively. In the best of circumstances, the individual can bend and not break when emotional situations arise. Falling back upon secure attachment paradigms, such fortunate people feel reasonably secure and confident. In more unfortunate situations, the individual feels inundated and responds with the coping methods available, even if these significantly compromise functioning. The implicit but compelling need is always to make the best of a bad situation, even though the best is not always as beneficial as we would hope.

PART THREE

CAN I BE DIFFERENT THAN I HAVE ALWAYS BEEN? IF SO, HOW?

I been in sorrow's kitchen and I done licked the pots clean.

—Florida folk saying

Everyone who visits a therapist does so because of the conscious desire to feel better, to rid oneself of sorrow and despair. On the other hand, most, because their psychic solutions are the best they can achieve, are wary of change. The dilemma of wanting to feel better while remaining the same is a formidable obstacle in therapy. Yet it is within these resistances, conscious and otherwise, that the patient can find the pathway to change. Therapeutically approaching the resistances, and the anxieties beneath, opens access to what may feel to be problematic and intractable aspects of character structure.

The previous chapters on character structure, and its various components, give a good basis for now tackling the next task: describing methods of confronting conflict therapeutically—helping patients to find alternative ways of thinking and feeling about themselves and about others. A wonderful outcome of therapy is when psychic adhesions release and the patient feels freer to find more satisfaction in life. Another outcome is to enable patients to come to grips with shortcomings—their own and those of others—is enormously freeing. From this, one can then move on from unmanageable conflict to more comfortable accommodation with the inevitable complexities and complications of life.

CHAPTER SEVEN

Therapeutic Interventions

As we know, I have divided the therapeutic enterprise of assessment and intervention for ease of discussion. But it is clear that assessment and treatment are necessarily and importantly intertwined. Important interactions occur from the moment the two participants connect, each simultaneously assessing the other, on multiple levels. Emotional tones and relationship maneuvers occur right from the beginning. Throughout the course of the therapy, the therapist and patient are fruitfully engaged in an ongoing process of understanding and intervention. Neither exists independently.

In this chapter I will explore how the therapist proceeds to use the dynamic picture of the patient to make observations and interpretations toward the goal of diminishing conflict.

Context vs. Content

The understanding of character structure and its various components stands as a foundation or touchstone that gives shape and meaning to the day-to-day work of the therapy. This conception of the patient's internalizations, defenses, conflicts, etc., provides a *context* from which the patient's associations or *content* can be better comprehended. The more data or content (thoughts, feelings, fantasies, etc.) that the patient can make available, the more access the therapist has, and can then make relevant and meaningful interventions.

After the initial formulation where I introduce my conception of the patient's psychology, I may suggest a metaphor: that aspects of character structure (the context) can be considered akin to the chapter title of a book of the patient's personality. The content, the associations during the session, can be likened to the text of the chapter. I may bring forth this metaphor of chapter and text in order to emphasize how moment-to-moment thoughts, feelings, dreams, behaviors, etc., need, first, to be examined in great detail (as one might carefully peruse the prose of a book) in order to grasp the elaborate intricacy of the psyche and, second, to place them in context (chapter titles) of their character structure. Of course I also know that this process is not so straightforward and without peril; the defenses allied against openness are formidable and important to explore and understand in their own right, and I am not ignoring that aspect of the therapeutic process but I am educating the patient that the alternation between context and content is an effective curative path.

Here is an example of how I conceive of the context-content relationship: I have given an extensive formulation of Marie's dynamics in previous chapters. This formulation—a picture of her character structure, and of its components—provides the context from which her thoughts and feelings can be seen as pieces of the overall picture of her personality. As we know Marie is conflicted over angry feelings; in fact, at times she does not realize that she is furious. Instead she might feel depressed or anxious, and it is only under close attention that we are able to find the truer feelings motivating the symptoms. After one such depressive incident, I requested that Marie tell me in detail the incidents of the previous day. As I have said earlier, the patient's "free associations" or associations to a dream, or gaps in associating, often provide a pathway into the patient's unconscious. Symptoms do not derive out of the ether; inevitably they arise from some stimuli (another type of context) in the environment (in dream analysis we refer to this as "day residue"). Marie tells me about a close friend's rather critical opinions about Marie's children. In the past Marie had only thought her friend to be helpful; now she wondered whether her friend Laurie was other than that. As we discussed this, Marie became red in the face, tearful and really angry. She then realized that she had shut out of awareness her true feelings about Laurie and her negativity. As we discussed this, she became cognizant that Laurie's negativity was not that different from that of her parents, and her disavowal now matched the disavowal that she had used throughout her life as a way to consciously mitigate the hurt she suffered from her parents' attitudes. All of this everyday material (content) is tied into the picture of her character structure (context) and she begins to see how the disavowal of feelings, in this case in particular, and, as a general defensive style is part and parcel of her character structure. The back and forth movement between interpreting content and then context allows the patient to feel well grounded in seeing how present-day matters relate not only to history but also to character structure. Conflict and Marie's concerns with it, is seen not only in isolation but also in terms of a broader context.

Empathy

Empathy and sympathy are not synonymous. Both activities are essential in therapy but empathy is much more personal, and at times, harder to achieve. This is what I said about it previously: "Empathy is not the same as sympathy; it demands more intimate involvement and more rigorous understanding. This is not to devalue sympathy, or to imply that it is always easy. It can be hard to feel for a patient when he or she behaves unkindly, for example, or acts in ways that go against one's own most deeply held ethical convictions. But empathy demands an active suspension of judgment, and an openness to the other person's experience that can be very difficult to achieve" (Hooberman, 2007, 29). It is an ideal in therapy to be totally empathic; and yet as any ideal, worthwhile to work toward, but impossible to achieve. Yet failures in empathy are not necessarily detrimental (Kohut, 1971) and can result in an enactment, a collision between two psyches. The outcome if handled well will become therapeutic; if handled poorly it may not only repeat earlier traumas (of each participant) but original problematic outcomes as well. Enactments emerge from the unconscious and happen spontaneously and without volition. Enactments don't only happen in therapy, but with others in one's life as well. Helping patients to become empathic to their contributions to conflict is essential, but it is just as important for one to be empathic to the other's unconscious activities that contribute to the discord as well (this is especially relevant in marital matters).

Often we hear of the therapeutic value of empathy. But we should ask the question: "Empathic to what?" In other words, at what level should one be empathic toward? The manifest? The underlying motivating force? The anxiety? An example: Lois tells me that she doesn't want to come to the session next week. She's a teacher and is out for winter break and "is too busy" to come. I suggest perhaps another reason. She says no, she just is too busy. As she leaves I am under the impression she'll be in next week but am prepared for an absence.

The next week, on the day of the session, she leaves a message informing me that she won't be in, indicating a fever. Obviously I am skeptical. In the next session I bring this up and she acknowledges that she lied—she didn't want to come and lying "seemed easier." "Why easier?" I wonder. She doesn't know and she doesn't want to talk about it. I don't respond. After a moment or two, she wonders how I feel. I ask her how she would feel if someone lied to her. "Hurt and angry." I nod in assent. She then sarcastically asks, "Do you want me to apologize? Do you want to yell at me?" I don't answer but do suggest we should wonder what is going on. Why was she so dogged in her determination to not only not come to the session, but to do so in a way that puts us at odds, inviting me to be punitive? As she continues to speak, she describes how lonely she is, particularly during vacation; others have spouses and families and she does not. She hates their happiness. "Does that include mine?" I wonder. She spits out a vituperative "Yes!" I can see that the holiday season is difficult for her, but still wonder why she needs to make me mad. At this point I am empathic to her pain, but what else resides beneath the surface? She and I also know that she was raised in an atmosphere where sadness and disappointment were not well tolerated; instead anyone showing such "weakness" was derided. Lois came upon the compromise formation to fabricate physical pain as a way of avoiding psychic pain. In her family, parents and siblings would argue, often fudging the truth, creating strong negative emotions, allowing some discharge of emotion, without divulging the secret of psychic pain.

She knew no other way of expressing her envy and resentment toward me, and she sadistically also wanted me to feel pain as she did. Yet she felt guilty for her lying and for her hostility and "wanted" to invoke a punitive response from me, relieving the guilt through a "beating." But there is still more. She has strong attachment and sexual desires toward me, and she tries to create an emotional interchange between us, albeit negative, to at least have some contact with me. This hostility is gratifying sadomasochistically but evokes more guilt, and more maneuvering to manage the guilt. The more we discuss, the more layers of meaning we find; all of which gives me more opportunities to be empathic and nonjudgmental, which allows her to use reflective functioning and mentalizing (for her to be empathic to my position) and then to find new understanding and new strategies to work through her pains and conflicts.

So we can see that empathy doesn't mean only feeling for the patient on the manifest ("upstairs") level, but on the hidden ("downstairs" including unconscious fantasies), levels that are generally more exquisitely sensitive and consequently in need of greater tenderness, understanding and concern. Let me emphasize, though, that I would be remiss If I were not being empathic to, first, my own need to maintain a boundary in the therapy and, second, to my humanness as well, in realizing that I am not immune from feeling hurt and angry when subjected to hostility.

Observation

Those of us in the psychotherapy profession are typically intense observers of the human condition. And this quality stands us in good stead in our work since it is essential to be a rapt observer of the patient, ourselves, and of our relationship. What we observe is the data that we use to understand (character structure or context and content of the moment, implicit level of organization, central fantasies, etc.) that in turn opens the door to intervention. How do we observe?

In the example above, I am aware of Lois's behavior (lying and provocation), her feeling states (anger and sadness), my feeling states (initial hurt and anger) and the differing quality of relationship (from contentiousness to cooperative and warm). So as therapists we try to be highly attuned to affective states, expressed and not expressed, to body posture, to feeling tone (atmosphere), to changes in affect, to silences, to gaps in thoughts, to sequence of thoughts, to unusual use of words or of oddity of sentence structure, to the theme of the session and narrative flow. Since there is so much to observe, I cannot deliver an exhaustive list. But I do want to emphasize that I am not solely referring to the patient in the list of what is observed. I observe myself no less than I do my patients. The therapist is simultaneously keeping track (observing) of his reactions as much as those of the patient. From these observations, the astute therapist verbalizes what he feels might be meaningful to the patient in order to move the therapy along. And of course the clinician is especially tuned into matters of conflict.

There is a direct connection between conscious and unconscious aspects, and close observation is essential in capturing the fullest extent of the patient's personality. Now of course, an observation is always the beginning of any intervention but one type of intervention is to verbalize the observation, without delving into underlying motivating material, similar to when I ask patients to "observe and report." One point that is important to remember: There are a myriad number of mental activities that transpire from session to session. The particular material that the patient chooses to discuss is always meaningful to observe, at the very least, and to comment upon when appropriate.

Maggie often felt unsettled or had trouble sleeping but was puzzled as to the precipitants. Listening to her associations and making observations of the sequence of her thoughts often put her in touch with the underlying causes. After one of those sleepless nights, she described taking a trip with a relative, Sue, and felt it went well; she had a good time. I asked for more details. Maggie told me that Sue has the habit of retiring for bed at eight, and rising in the morning at five. Also, she walked out of restaurants if she had to wait more than a few minutes for a table. I then only repeated what I observed, that she had trouble sleeping and that the next thing that she told me about was Sue's odd habits. Maggie immediately became intensely emotional, speaking with great vigor about Sue's "weirdness," and how her relative's behavior was too reminiscent of her family and their dysfunction. Later we will have more opportunity to delve deeper into more hidden feelings and fantasies. But by my observing and reporting, Maggie becomes aware of the link between her sleeplessness and the intense feelings about Sue and, by extension, her family.

Affirmation

Many people are desperately in need of feeling soothed and salved in the midst of conflict and turmoil. One of the essential goals of therapy is for the patient to be able to find the means of self-soothing. When accomplished this will strengthen the internal resources required to face conflictual matters. The first step in this is for the therapist to provide an atmosphere of affirmation. By affirmation I mean responding not just empathically to a patient but also with a positive and genuine sense of appreciation. Kohut (1971) emphasized the importance of parents positively "mirroring" the child's expressive needs and wrote of the importance of mirror transferences in therapy. "In this . . . sense of the term the mirror transference is the therapeutic reinstatement of that normal phase of the development of the grandiose self in which the gleam in the mother's eye, which mirrors the child's exhibitionistic display . . . confirm the child's self-esteem . . ." (117). From the developmental perspective, a child's cohesive self derives, in part, from the internalization of the positive and loving gazes (parent as mirror) from the parent to the child. It should be remembered that the outcome of a parental gaze that is predominantly critical, shaming or guilt inducing is the development of negative self-evaluations, and if severe enough creates false, empty or fragmented selves.

Effective mirroring and affirmation by the therapist assists, first of all, in the patient replacing negative self-evaluative aspects with more positive ones derived from the therapist's more benign attitude, and smoothes the path toward deeper understanding as the patient feels (on an implicit level) that he is safe (see below) in divulging tender and vulnerable facets of the self. All of this stands in good stead when deeper and more difficult areas of conflict are attended to.

How does one establish an affirmative tone in the interpretive work? One rule of thumb is to "interpret up instead of down." For instance, I can emphasize that Lois's primary desire in cancelling is to hurt me sadistically ("down") or I can recognize that her behavior represents her striving to find a way to communicate to me an intense feeling of hurt and shame, and a wish for me to understand that she is limited in her ways of processing hurt ("up"). Interpreting "up" means appreciating the underlying feelings of hurt and the need for love and nurturance; interpreting "down" means identifying desires to damage and humiliate. Each type of intervention has its place, but a more positive take recognizes that hostility derives originally from narcissistic injury (the need to hurt is not primary), and tends to encourage more self-disclosure as one does not feel "caught" because of "bad behavior."

Another aspect of affirmation is the importance of conveying to the patient that the therapist is not only empathic to the patient's struggles but also likes and respects him as a person. This is not always easy as we may find facets of the patient that run contrary to our moral standards, or the patient may push our emotional buttons. Most clinicians genuinely wish to help their patients and are sympathetic and empathetic to their plight. Sometimes we might take it for granted that our patients know this, yet they often do not as they are beset by terribly strong self-criticisms and cannot imagine that others do not share them. Therapists can go a long way in creating a warm and accepting atmosphere by verbally conveying appreciation and admiration for the patient and for various personality characteristics.

When I worked with violent criminals in the prison system, I soon realized that I couldn't make much headway if my response to them contained an equally violent distaste for what were oftentimes terrible violations of humanity. I needed to emphasize with myself and with them that my job was not to judge but to try to maintain a sense of acceptance for their humanity. This is in marked contrast to their experiences throughout life that were filled with brutality and abuse. To accomplish the often difficult task of being accepting, I would empathically focus on their emotional pain as well as on other causative factors leading to their violent behavior. In this I am providing emotional support and intellectual understanding (formulation) of their character structure and their deficiencies in conflict resolution. Yet, at the same time I need to not excuse or justify their actions but also to help them come to terms with behavior that most often they too felt was reprehensible—again, a need to maintain empathy about different levels of psychic activity and behavior.

In some instances, patients view the therapeutic situation as not much different from the confessional, and they have a need to receive some sort of absolution for misdeeds. But the object of therapy is not to give the therapist the power to punish or to forgive; it is to help the patient to view her behavior in context of her character structure, and with the help of the therapist, to find a way to process shameful acts in a fashion that is less self-punishing and more empathic to oneself. As badly as a person may feel for some actions that feel reprehensible, the individual may want to focus on her "badness" instead of other matters that might feel more painful (Lois would rather that I punish her than for us to examine her abject loneliness). Therapists are best served in any given session to listen carefully for themes to emerge, and then to address the prevailing psychic pressure that emerges. In this fashion, the therapist can let the need for self-punishment fall to the side, in order to address more compelling matters. As I will elucidate in the next chapter, we will not ignore any aspect of patient behavior, including those that show the person in a less than flattering light, but we will do so within the context of the situation and of character structure, and in an affirming and empathic fashion.

Reframing

The close relative of affirmation is the action of reframing, that is, helping the patient see that his characteristic way of viewing himself is not set in stone, but that other perspectives are often more nuanced and more apropos to the situation. Len, who has given both of us fits with his sleepiness, has made some nascent moves toward being more talkative. Yet he still bemoans his many difficulties—his weight, his indecision about his marriage, and his lassitude at work. In reframing I tell him that I understand his frustration, but that he needs also to recognize the progress that he has made, both in life and in our therapy. First of all, I indicate, that for someone coming from his abusive background, he is quite successful (and he is, having risen to a position of prominence in his company). And although he has trouble associating, he has made some inroads in this regard, and that we need to recognize that his difficulty in being more connected in the therapy is a consequence of his traumatic background, and not a personal shortcoming. Finally, I point out to him that he is courageous and diligent in our work together and that speaks well of his character. The reframing replaces a sense of failure with a more positive position, reduces anxiety and opens more doors of inquiry into his internal world, and this in turn helps him to feel more open to address that which he finds so terrifying to confront.

Reframing isn't only about finding positive qualities of a patient where negative ones seem inevitable. It is also the process of pointing out relevant aspects of a situation that have been denied, ignored or simply not previously available for understanding.

Safety

A sense of safety in the therapeutic relationship only comes about from the dialectic between the patient's anxiety over self-disclosure and the therapist's desire to provide an environment that is warm, encouraging, positive, empathic and that operates within a consistent therapeutic frame. Empathy, affirmation, affection, mirroring and respect for the individual all culminate in the patient feeling safe in confronting areas of exquisite sensitivity. And this occurs within the context of the therapist delivering what is implicitly promised—a relationship that is based on trust and commitment and a therapy that provides understanding of anxieties that have felt beyond the ken of the patient to resolve.

Feeling safe is hard for anyone; feeling safe when one has a history of emotional disappointment is another matter. The sense of safety increases through a variety of experiences in a caring environment: where unhelpful defenses are gradually set aside; when the sense of collaboration between therapist and patient deepens concomitantly; when enactments and other emotional interchanges are handled with sensitivity; where transference and countertransferences are addressed and dealt with. As with any relationship, the personal connection intensifies over time and through experiences, both easy and hard.

Ken, age fifty-four, came to me seeking assistance in his ongoing relationship problems with women. His history was quite unfortunate, including physical and emotional abuse at the hands of his mother, and neglect from both parents. Older cousins were sexually abusive when he visited his extended family during the summer. Although not totally abandoned, he had to fend for himself often during his younger childhood years and regularly took a consoling and care-taking role with his mother after his father left the family. He had been married and divorced twice but had remained on good terms with his former wives and had been a positive figure for his own children and those of his exes. Despite his unfavorable upbringing he had the wherewithal to gain an education and to work successfully as a counselor at a facility for acting out adolescents. Ken was no pushover to be sure, but he felt strongly for the kids under his purview and seemed to me to provide them with just the right mixture of affection, understanding and hard-nosed discipline.

He had tried several therapists prior to our meeting and found that they "meant well" but that he did not feel that he made much progress. I was immediately struck with several of his personality characteristics. First, despite his history of abuse, he was quite warm and emotionally available. Secondly, he had a wide network of friends who valued his company. Third, he had a good mind and was able to make good use of reflective thinking. Further I felt moved by the degree of psychic pain that he had endured, then and now.

Ken had an intellectual understanding that his background affected both his moods and relationships but still could not find that elusive "something" that would enable him to venture more safely into relationships. I was immediately alerted to the fact that he was not likely to feel particularly safe with me either. And why should he? Thus far important people had let him down (including previous therapists). Why should he trust me over anyone else?

The less traumatized need to feel a sense of acceptance and understanding in the initial phases of therapy, to be sure. But with those with a background like Ken's it is all the more essential to address this as soon as possible, as it is easy to quickly lose the patient's confidence. I told Ken this, indicating that I could well understand any hesitation or reluctance he had in both continuing in therapy and in being able to let down his guard in order to gain access to troubling anxieties and conflicts. I informed him that it would take time for us to get to know each other to attain a greater level of comfort. I also said that while we knew the general areas of sensitivity within his mind, we still had a long way to go to understand specifically what was behind (unconscious reasons, fantasies, etc.) his discomfort with relationships. But I was confident that we could do so, over time. I also told him that I felt that his accomplishments were quite impressive.

Over two months of weekly sessions, we explored his present-day relationships and I made suggestions as to the underlying reasons for his avoidant reactions. I told him that he was understandably fearful that any relationship would end up like those of his childhood, exploitative and profoundly disappointing. At that point, after some rapport was established, Ken anxiously told me that he was concerned about an aspect of our relationship. I encouraged him to talk about it. He said that he perceived that I came from a more "upscale" world than he did, and he wondered whether I would be able to understand and appreciate his different cultural background. This sounds rather benign, and was to me, but he said it in a rather bombastic style, in a way that some might consider challenging. I didn't feel threatened or annoyed; instead I was empathic to his concern. I indicated that it was true that I did come from a more privileged background but that, with his help, I felt that I would be able to understand his points of view. He wanted to know if I was mad for his challenging attitude. "On the contrary," I told him. "I'm delighted that you told me your concern and hope that you will continue to tell me what is on your mind." He felt quite relieved and I felt that the therapeutic alliance had taken hold. In a session not long after, he was greatly conflicted about whether to continue dating an old flame. I asked him to describe her, and eventually I asked if she seemed depressed. "Of course," he answered. I told him that I thought that, despite liking her a great deal, that he might be worried about getting involved with a woman who, like his mother, had emotional difficulties. "Wow, I guess so," he responded. Now this is no great shakes of an incisive interpretation, but it gained traction because he felt safe enough to be open in order to consider what may have seemed obvious. I don't doubt that previous therapists might have made the same observation, but it was his trust and sense of safety that allowed him to take my observation in.

A sense of safety develops over time and relates to a number of factors. Some of which are: that ephemeral "good fit" between patient and therapist, the therapist's ability to be empathic and sympathetic, the patient's sense that he is understood, the openness demonstrated by the therapist, a cooperative and collaborative attitude—the notion that the two participants are equal (even if the necessary asymmetry is present in the therapeutic relationship), a sense that no thought or feeling is out of bound, including conflicts or enactments within the therapy and that the therapist is ready and willing to deal with any eventuality that might arise in the treatment. It is still relatively early in Ken's treatment but we are well on the way toward delving into areas of conflict that he knows he needs to confront which heretofore have felt unavailable because of the terror they elicit.

Educative

We've had a bit of a preview in describing the educative aspect of psychotherapy in my discussions on upstairs-downstairs and on context vs. content. One can say that any intervention made by a therapist is educative in the sense that one is informing the patient of something not previously known. But there is a distinction between informing a patient of what may be considered to be more "factual" aspects of human functioning versus an interpretation of specific not previously understood facets of an individual's internal world (McWilliams, 2003, expounds nicely on this topic).

There are many factual matters that are conveyed to a patient. Obviously we can start with the therapist's ground rules—length of sessions, payment issues, cancellation policy and such. Other helpful educative work revolves around description of the manner in which psychotherapy works, i.e., free association, the importance of linking past with present, how present-day relationships (including the transference) connect with past childhood relationships. Although these may seem obvious to the more sophisticated consumer of therapy, it is wise to not assume that patients have these matters available and I inform all patients of these actualities. Another educative aspect is the formulation process whereby we enlighten patients as to aspects of their inner worlds and how they relate to present-day symptoms. McWilliams points out that therapists often convey information on the process of personality development and of the ways in which minds typically function in dealing with stress.

I have also found that it can be quite helpful to educate patients on issues such as the importance of being reflective and of using their mind in a thoughtful way. Earlier I promised that I would describe how Len and I were able to make some inroads in what seemed to be an impenetrable mind. There were several factors that helped in our accomplishment: continued empathy, a gradual developing sense of trust and safety through my steadfast interest in him (affirmation) and in his mind, and a professed certainty that he would be helped. But also I took a rather unusual step to engage Len in more thoughtful inquiry. At one point in discussing reflective thought, I asked him what he thought about when he was driving in his car to and from work. He said that he tried not to think. I gently told him that if that was his goal, he was successful but didn't think that was a good strategy long term. He acknowledged that he could see that. "What do you listen to on the radio?" I wondered. "Sports talk radio," he answered. I indicated to him that perhaps another listening source might be helpful. He asked for suggestions. I then told him about NPR, describing several of their shows that were on our local stations. He seemed intrigued. In the next few weeks, he started listening to NPR, and he discussed various topics that he found of interest. Those that he brought to therapy for discussion always had some relation to a matter close to home. I was glad to hear that he alternated listening to Public Radio with sports stations as I hoped that he would not change his habits out of compliance with my wishes. I am not the rabid sports fan that he is but I can hold my own in a discussion on current sports events and that too was helpful in developing rapport. I took pains to be open to discussing any issues of interest to him, often being satisfied with a give and take conversation without making any interpretive statements, content to further our reflections.

As time went on he started to bring questions about child-raising to our sessions and he found that I was a good navigator in what he perceived as the treacherous waters of being a father. He fervently loved his children and did not want them to have the same kind of disastrous relationship as he had with his father (past abuse and presently he had no contact with him), and he relished my input.

All of these experiences contributed to Len becoming much more open and communicative. Since talking freely then became more the rule than the exception we could look for thoughts, feelings or fantasies that might be defended against when his yawning recurred. We began to hone in on his tremendous fear of being alone, and the conflict between this fear and his desire to become more independent took center stage. Empathy, providing a sense of safety, establishing a strong therapeutic relationship, educating him to various aspects of his mind and his confidence in me and in the process led us to a therapy that was now far more vital and alive than previously.

Developing a Narrative

Patients all have stories that they want and need to tell. An important aspect of any treatment is to encourage patients to develop a narrative that connects the dots, so to speak, of their lifelong experiences and their own sense of their development. As Spence (1982) points out one cannot confirm that the narrative "truth" corresponds to "historical truth" (remember my discussion on soccer parents and constructions). Nevertheless it is a fruitful activity for therapist and patient to develop a story that largely identifies and explains aspects of the patient's life and psyche in a fashion that logically and intuitively makes sense.

Earlier in this book I described the intensity of desire to satisfy unconscious central fantasies. Part of the development of a narrative is to identify these fantasies and to put them in context with the patient's thrust to find meaning in life. The narrative includes conscious, preconscious and unconscious fantasies, to the extent that they are knowable and become known through the treatment.

From my description of Marie (and other patients) we can see that we are developing a narrative of her life and psyche. As we delve deeper and broader into her internal world, she has a "story" of her life at hand, one that she can refer to in the midst of conflict and which can then give her a sense of both understanding and security. The narrative continues to evolve, as more information becomes available, and all of this provides sturdiness to her character structure.

Interpretation

In my last book (Hooberman, 2007) I wrote about interpretations. "I define an interpretation as a verbal interchange between therapist and patient that provides an explanation for feeling, thought, memory or action, whether consciously noticed or not" (2). Clearly I am not interested in offering another comprehensive treatise on interpretation here, but I will endeavor to touch upon some crucial matters to consider in fashioning interpretations toward conflict resolution.

Interpretation is often considered the sine qua non of psychotherapy, holding other interventions in lower esteem. I disagree with this as all of the actions that I have already discussed can have profound effects on patients. Yet, without doubt many important interventions are directed toward explaining behavior, thoughts and actions (the definition of an interpretation), the underpinnings of conflict.

How can a therapist sort through the thicket of associations—thoughts, feelings, fantasies, dreams, unexpressed but atmospheric senses—all of the aspects that are presented in a session, in order to deliver an interpretation that is both salient and helpful?

Typically patients unconsciously (or sometimes consciously) organize their thoughts into loosely knit themes that emerge during the session. That is why it is often best for therapists to wait for the dominant theme to emerge prior to making an intervention. The therapist uses his knowledge of the patient's inner world (formulation) and listens (observes) for what he feels are the most pressing issues to be addressed. Therapists eventually learn to trust their intuition, combined with knowledge of the patient to identifying these salient matters. For instance, with a patient who tends to disavow feeling it would not be unusual for me to say something like, "I know that you are saying that you are angry, but I really sense that you are feeling more sad and disappointed than mad." I use whatever material I have available in order to fashion an interpretation—my overall sense of the patient, my feelings in the moment, the nature of the material being presented (content, sequences, associations) and the general direction that the treatment has been moving.

I mentioned interpreting "up" instead of "down" as one rule of thumb in relation to interpretive choice. Langs (1979) has other suggestions: ". . . here is a series of hierarchies of indications for interventions, which I would state as follows: resistance before content, interactional resistance before intrapsychic resistance, defense before content, framework before all other material (content or defense), medium before content, communicative style before content, reality before fantasy, analyst before patient" (29). In essence Langs is indicating that any interpretative process is more palatable if it proceeds from surface to depth and from less threatening to more, over time. None of these suggestions are hard and fast—rather the therapist faces decision points throughout the therapy, when and how to deliver an interpretation. In general, though, it is the job of the therapist to identify areas of conflict and to then deliver an interpretation (explanation) that is palatable to the patient (with the understanding that enactments and disagreements are inevitable), is emotionally vibrant and not intellectualized (by intellectualized I mean perhaps "correct" but devoid of affect) and makes sense within the context of the therapy and the personality of the patient.

I am going to divide my brief discussion on the interpretive activity into different foci, with the familiar caveat that the distinctions are not hard and fast but are presented in this fashion for clarity. First I will address interpretations that emphasize understanding underlying meaning, and then those that concentrate on identifying underlying motivation. I will then discuss interpretations regarding the therapeutic relationship. I am addressing these issues from the perspective of how best to approach conflict and its vicissitudes.

Meaning

Killingmo (1989) and Tuch (2007) both suggest that patients who lean toward less reflective thinking and more concreteness often do better with interpretations that emphasize the meaning of their thoughts and associations without imputing any sense of responsibility for their actions. These individuals are those who tend to view some therapist activities from the "paranoid" position, i.e., feeling threatened and attacked by interventions when they may feel blamed for their predicament. As Killingmo states, "it is not a matter of defending oneself against anxiety connected with bad intentions, e.g., forbidden, object-directed needs, fantasies and feelings, as is the case in [neurotic or less disturbed] conflict. What is defended against is primarily anxiety of fragmentation, i.e., losing one's own sense of identity" (brackets added, 67). Clearly one must tread carefully lest psychic deterioration occur.

But while caution is called for with the more severely disturbed, it is important in any treatment to keep in mind the tender psyches of all patients. Everyone is threatened by the notion that they will be blamed for the predicaments they find themselves in. Interpretations in this "meaning" modality are made about material that resides in the conscious or preconscious—or in my lexicon, in the implicit level of consciousness.

When I tell Len that he is reenacting his bedtime ritual with me (by yawning and creating a sleepy atmosphere), I am providing him with a sense of *meaning* of his behavior that previously he had been unaware. When it first came up I did not suggest that he is intending to do anything to me; rather I am helping him see the correspondence between present and past. In doing so I am supporting our work in the therapy by suggesting that his behavior is beyond his conscious control—that it is inevitable that individuals repeat in the present that which they experienced in the past. Just as he did not invite the abuse in the past, he is not consciously "trying" to create discomfort for me. This interpretation provides relief, as he does not feel the need to self-attack since I am empathizing with the effects of his abusive and neglectful parents. The interpretation works toward strengthening his ego by crystallizing amorphously understood behavior into something more concrete and understandable. He can now say to himself, "I am sleepy not because I am bad but because of my bad experiences in childhood." When Len encounters difficult situations (conflict) he can now understand that his reactions of anxiety, withdrawal or extreme anger derive from the fact that he experiences the present-day situation as being similar to traumatic events in the past. Although this type of intervention is not completely curative for Len, it is quite helpful and prepares him for more intensive work.

Our next interpretive step is to assist him to see how the sleepiness has tendrils that reach down into his unconscious, is used defensively, and represents hidden fantasies and desires.

Motivation

Attributing underlying wishes to patients can be fraught. Some feel accused, caught for some kind of wrongdoing; others feel embarrassed and ashamed. Still others, those who have been beaten for alleged misdeeds are extremely reluctant to "admit" to any perceived desires, believing that awareness of them will lead toward intense feelings of badness. In this regard in my previous life as a prison psychologist, I was struck by prisoners' dogmatic protestations of innocence, especially in front of the Parole Board who mostly were interested in hearing some sense of contrition. Instead, forever fearing intense, self-destructive and fragmenting consequences, the men would do anything to avoid accepting responsibility even if it meant continued incarceration.

As the imputation of responsibility carries such risk, it is essential that the therapist work diligently at creating an atmosphere of trust, safety, empathy, affirmation and compassion. From there we can venture into more treacherous waters. Interpretations about motivation are often about *hidden* motivation. Thus interpretations in this modality concern material in the preconscious and unconscious levels of personality.

Identifying defense before content is often the first step in this type of work. Laura, a college student, had multiple problems with affect regulation and had significant difficulty in getting to work or classes on a regular basis. I would often try to figure out the precipitants of her depressive spikes but even when I could, making the connection between stimuli and response never seemed to go anywhere. She would lament that she was a failure if she only could get four out of eight problems on her advanced physics exam. I pointed out to her that she was able to get four; that seemed admirable in and of itself. But, why didn't she go to class and figure out what she was doing incorrectly? This was unacceptable to her; she was an abysmal failure, she lamented. I told her that the constant self-abnegation was a result of her internalized self-representations (not in those technical terms though) and also operated as a defense, since the constant self-criticism stood in the way of pondering what I had to say or to free associate in order to help us find the underpinnings of her difficulty in concentrating on her studies.

She had a history of sexual abuse and overstimulation. I pointed out to her that the desire to not "see" aspects of those experiences became generalized into the present when she would not allow herself to "see" the paths toward solutions of her physics problems. This interpretation was helpful in that she could understand that her concern over being overwhelmed in the past was actually contributing to being overwhelmed in the present. Further, by opening herself to more openness of thought, she could use her mind more productively. I am attributing a motivation to her behavior—a desire to negate the reality of past abuse, brought into her contemporary life. We can then move on to explore her feelings toward me that frighten her because of the confusion between closeness and sexuality. There is certainly more to understand though—her need to sabotage herself, her anxiety over success, her feelings of entitlement to get perfect grades regardless of her skill level or the amount of time spent studying, and of course repressed memories of her abuse. Inquiries into these areas will come as her defenses soften and when she feels more comfortable with the notion that she is the author of her own life's drama.

Let's take a closer look at Len. I have established that his yawning is connected with his past bedtime experiences with his mother, and this is helpful as far as it goes. When we approach material that is threatening, Len begins to yawn, attempting to dissociate from fearful thoughts and feelings (much like his mother's dissociative disorder). After he feels safer and more able to use his mind reflectively, I introduce the notion that his yawning also operates as a defense. I suggest to him that he tends to start yawning when we approach material that he finds threatening. At this point he is intrigued, and we wonder together what may lay underneath that is so concerning. I suggest to him that he must be intensely worried since, along with his yawning, his seemingly intractable overeating is so extreme (the severity of the symptom indicates the severity of the trauma). He agrees. Here I am interpreting that the yawning and overeating are motivated by his desire to defend against painful memories and affects. By this time Len feels sufficiently safe and able to reflect upon his own thoughts such that he can tolerate an attribution of motive. I address this below.

If we can go back to the context-content paradigm that I earlier introduced, we can see that the distinction between interpretations based on meaning versus those on motivation fits well into that schema. Interpretations on meaning focus more on general patterns of functioning even if we are discussing the specifics of a reaction (such as with Len above, and his sleepiness) while interpretations about motivation relate more directly to a matter at hand, conflict in action in day-to-day life.

Transformation through the Therapeutic Relationship[1]

Therapy consists of a relationship and effective therapy makes use of the relationship as a potent therapeutic agent. As a relationship, therapy is intensely meaningful to the therapist as well. And well it should be since a good therapist is putting his or her emotions on display as well; a committed therapeutic relationship is no different from any other, with rewards equal to the emotional risk. The therapeutic relationship is the most potent therapeutic tool we have available. It provides fertile soil for conflicts to emerge with full emotional force that can then be examined in detail.

I am dividing my discussion of the therapeutic relationship into two: the first having to do with more traditional notions of transference-countertransference, and the second with affectively alive interactions between therapist and patient.

Transference-Countertransference

Let's continue the discussion on Len and his yawning to illuminate transference and countertransference issues. Len remembers little of his childhood. But we strongly suspect that he was, at the very least sexually overstimulated, if not a victim of outright sexual abuse. From his report two of his sisters vaguely (an unfortunate family trait) remembered that their father was sexually inappropriate. Len asked another sister more specifically of her knowledge of sexual abuse and she indicated that she was certain it occurred but that she could not recapture any memories. This same sister reported that he was present when his father "groped" their mother, and when he walked around nude in front of his children. Len remembers neither of these activities. It was also known to Len and his sisters that his father was sexually abused by his father.

Feeling a bit at sea because of Len's memory gaps, I suggested that his mother come to a session to provide more background. She kindly came and acknowledged not only her dissociative disorder but also her own sexually traumatic background, having been abused by her father. Consistent with her dissociative diagnosis Len's mother disavowed any knowledge of the verified physical abuse by father, and of any purported sexual abuse. She did indicate that she had known that both Len's father and grandfather engaged in cross-dressing. Len's mother also indicated that another son had intimated that something had happened with the father in a bathtub but he refused to discuss it further.

What Len does remember he does with no affect, defending against being overwhelmed and disorganized by the memory of vicious verbal, physical and sexual attacks via his father, and by the desperate feeling of confusion conveyed from his mother's alternation of distance and overstimulating closeness. The fear keeps him locked in a conflict between, on one hand, wanting to know historical "fact" and contemporary feelings and, on the other, wanting to keep his and my mind numb and "dumb." The conflict between his wishes for closeness and his fear of forbidden and overwhelming feelings has contributed greatly to his difficulty in reflective thinking, and I strongly suspect to his overeating.

At this point Len and I are well acquainted with the landscape of his internal world. He is still anxious certainly but is now much better equipped to tolerate interpretations that indicate that he is in charge of his actions. Now when he becomes sleepy I can interpret defense, and based on his associations I can interpret content. Len had a fortunate health insurance policy that enabled him to engage in a five-time-weekly psychoanalysis. Through this we felt quite connected to each other. As an indication of his feelings about separation and loss, he would often have difficulty in giving us access to his thoughts on Mondays (after the weekend break) and on Fridays (right before the break). On one particular Monday he seemed especially distant. I commented upon this and he started yawning. I knew that his mother was visiting that weekend. I asked about her visit. He was laconic. He then told me a dream. "I'm in a school, walking out and a fifteen-year-old girl comes up to me and wants to know if I'll go out with her. I can't believe it. I say to her, 'Don't you know how old I am? I'm thirty-five!'" I asked for his thoughts. He told me that he was surprised by the dream, almost as if it were real, kind of an altered state. I wonder silently if it does represent reality, i.e., sexual attraction between generations, between his father and him, and/or his mother and him. Altered states often point to a person struggling with a past experience that felt real and unreal at the same time.

Len becomes quiet. He pauses and then speaks briefly about his mother and how he was pleased that she got along with his kids, and then he yawns again. I pointed out the yawn, and told him that I thought there was a connection between his mother and the dream. The dream, I told him, is one of intergenerational sexual attraction. He yawns. I indicate that clearly he is anxious about the idea that parent-child sexuality was a reality in his family. He says that it makes sense, and that it feels correct. I then ask him what he makes of the fact that he yawns fairly often with me. He yawns again. At this point we are nearing the end of the session and I finish by saying that I thought that our relationship does bring forth memories of his bedtime sojourns with mother, and that it is likely that he and his mother probably had more intense feelings toward each other than previously acknowledged, and perhaps the same kind of dynamic is at play with us. After I say this, I can tell that he becomes much more emotionally present, and in confirmation he tells me that he feels quite tearful.

Here we can see that Len has a conflict between his positive feelings toward me and his wish to avoid them. To him they represent forbidden, confusing and painful feelings from childhood. The atmospheric memory of being with his mother and/or father is evoked by the analytic situation. He unconsciously fears being overwhelmed and subject to ego fragmentation should memories and feelings of sexual arousal emerge. The dynamics that plague Len throughout his life become activated by the therapy and then available for discussion and understanding in real time. Past relationships become known through the present-day relationships with the therapist.

Transference does not exist independently of countertransference. In earlier psychoanalytic times countertransference was viewed as a failure of the therapist in maintaining his own psychic health. Nowadays we think of countertransferences as being inevitable emotional responses of the therapist to the unconscious pull of the patient's unconscious. If I was not affected by his psychology, our therapy would be sterile and he would likely feel alone and abandoned by feelings that are too much to process. With me sharing in these feelings, we can operate collaboratively to understand the deep pain and distress that he feels, and he can feel fortified by my affective presence. We are in this together. Any conflict is best faced not alone.

Interactive

One of the most curative aspects of the therapeutic endeavor derives from the intensity of the therapeutic relationship. Stern et al. (1998) in a landmark article describe the process of "implicit relational knowing," a nonverbal interaction based on patterns of relating, a way of knowing what is transpiring in a given situation without conscious consideration—an automatic sense of the nature of a relationship. From this experience may evolve what they refer to as "moments of meeting":

> The therapist must use a specific aspect of his or her individuality that carries a personal signature. The two are meeting as persons relatively unhidden by their usual therapeutic roles, for that moment. Also, the actions that make up the "moment of meeting" cannot be routine, habitual or technical; they must be novel and fashioned to meet the singularity of the moment. Of course this implies a measure of empathy, an openness to affective and cognitive reappraisal, a signalled affect attunement, a viewpoint that reflects and ratifies that what is happening is occurring in the domain of the "shared implicit relationship," i.e., a newly created dyadic state specific to the participants. (919)

We can see that when achieved, this experience makes real concepts that might have only been understood in an intellectual fashion. Further, a "moment of meeting" serves to not only alter the nature of the relationship but alters facets of the participants as well. Thus it serves as a conduit toward mutual regulation, that allows the patient to know, in her bones, that she has the ability to have an important impact on someone near and dear to her (in marked contrast perhaps to her life up to this point).

Freud (1912) suggested that therapists should listen to patients with "evenly suspended attention" (111), to allow their unconscious minds to be accessible in order to understand the patient's unconscious (most contemporary writers refer to this as "evenly hovering attention"). Although this model is essential in therapeutic work, modern Relational theory suggests that the therapist is not a passive receiver but should be emotionally present with an "evenly hovering relatedness," ready to engage the patient in authentic interactions, which then allows unspoken and nonconscious relational patterns to emerge. This newer paradigm goes hand in hand with the intersubjective openness that I am referring to here.

During "moments of meeting" patient and therapist roles fall away to some extent and the interaction is of two equal and emotional participants striving to understand the nature of the encounter, and of their individual reactions. In this interaction the patient and the therapist as well can find a sense of safety and well being, understanding implicitly that each can be loving and angry, sensual and objective, playful and serious, to name a few possibilities. All of these experiences are growth inducing and conflict reducing by stretching the participants' psyches to include more options of thought, action and feeling.

Here is an example of another therapeutic interaction between James and me—with some similarity to the one I described earlier. (I discuss this example in Hooberman, 2008).

James, to remind the reader, sought out treatment in the midst of the throes of a relationship problem. He was plagued by excessive hand washing, and preoccupation with germs. As I have indicated, symptoms don't exist in isolation. His obsessions and compulsions were part and parcel of an overriding character style.

His wife had sexually rejected James. More recently, he had been involved with a woman whom he cared for but for whom he had no great sexual interest. Being smaller and more slender than he wished, he found his girlfriend, Sara, who was about his height and a greater weight, to not be the "girl of his dreams," although she was someone with whom he felt a great emotional bond. Right before he came to see me, he met someone for whom he fell for hard—Julie, a pretty, small, sexy and vivacious woman who was emotionally erratic and "high maintenance." Desiring both safety and warmth, on one hand, and sexual satisfaction on the other, he found himself in a pickle—involved with two women yet not committing to either. Sara was someone with whom he felt safe; Julie was someone with whom he felt excited. Both alluring, but in vastly different ways. He tried to juggle both, putting each in the position of vying for his love. As soon as one would become tired of his wavering and become more distant, he would panic and try to win her back. Eventually, he decided to throw his lot in with Julie (even though she had her own ambivalence about the relationship), but he still attempted to maintain Sara as his "safety." Furious, Sara cut off any contact. This served to increase his anxiety, as he now felt it crucial to "win Julie over," fearful of being alone and unloved. His panic over this was palpable, and I found myself feeling a bit anxious too. The treatment became less reflective, as his preoccupation in his thoughts and in our sessions (his obsessional personality in full flower) was on his strategies to win her, and a discussion over his underlying panic or on his commitment problems held no interest for him.

I realized that I felt pressured, and I wondered silently about my collusion in agreeing to discuss what I considered in some sense to be "superficial" (e.g., wondering about what her behavior might mean; strategies over his maneuvers to win her over, etc.) resulting from unspoken but strongly felt externalizations, instead of pursuing more of an examination of his internal conflicts.

Eventually, when he thought he had secured Julie, he calmed and, as a consequence of his reduction in anxiety and due to what I felt was his unconscious wish to avoid any further psychic distress, his desire to distance himself from any feelings toward me and to act out his rejection/commitment dynamics, he expressed interest in reducing his sessions from three to one or none. Again I found myself feeling somewhat anxious and felt compelled to "convince" him of the need to continue at the same frequency, which although I absolutely felt was in his best interest, needed to be explored and not coerced. We discussed this situation a bit, and I invited him to wonder about his desire to cut down or leave treatment. While he was wondering about that, I pondered what I could learn from my own affective experiences in the sessions. I then realized that I was feeling toward him what he had felt with Julie and Sara: an urgency to "win him over." In the next session, as the discussion came around to his questioning the value of the therapy, I told him of my experience of our interaction—that I was feeling pressure to get him to stay and that it was identical to experiences that he had had with both his recent girlfriends, but also in his early life, as his mother had been at times rejecting and humiliating. I also told him that it had felt hurtful to me for him to so precipitously alter the treatment, as if he was carelessly discarding something that he no longer needed. I wondered whether he had ever felt this way. He perked up considerably at this. Indicating that he felt badly that he had created this for me (although it was really cocreated), he associated to his ex-wife and discussed with much more emotion the pain and rejection he felt. This led to more discussion about his feelings about his size, his sense of humiliation about this, his fear that he wouldn't be needed by his loved ones, and other such experiences in past and present life. He had more difficulty in speaking of his feelings for me, and how he perceived that I felt about him—both of which were anxiety arousing. Yet, all in all, he became much more reflective, and the anxiety and pressure in the room diminished for both of us; we were able to continue the treatment as before.

By sharing my affective reaction we were able to find his underlying defended-against affect. The emotionality of our interaction not only brought his feelings to the fore but also cemented our relationship. This in turn enabled him to be able to see the conflict between his need for strength and autonomy and his desire to be loved and valued for who he was, and his fear of wishing that from me. Following this session, James and I had many sessions where he sobbed over the pain of his feelings of rejection and humiliation from his parents, and his yearning for love and acceptance. I was quite moved by all of this and became tearful as well. All of this was curative and allowed him to further his pursuit of finding a woman who was not only attractive but was also sensitive and genuinely loving.

The spontaneous outpouring of emotion from each of us was unbidden and also uncontrolled. We met each other emotionally. What was curative was the "meeting of the minds" and then a stepping back and reflecting on our interaction and its relevance to his struggles and conflicts. We were no longer at odds, but collaborative and cooperative.

Marital Therapy

Marital therapy requires neutrality; the therapist cannot favor one partner over another. Of course this is followed in the main, but enactments occur in this venue as in individual therapy. And the same technique is applicable; a pursuit to understand how the psyches in the room are evoking difficult feelings. This can become complicated but the numbers of psyches are not a disadvantage; instead of two people working on a problem, now we have three who can put their minds at work to solve a conflict.

As I have described with Luke and Marie, marital therapy is designed to first identify family patterns of relating via identifications and to help the partners see how these representations are being externalized onto the relationship. The same context-content outlook is relevant here. In this situation we not only look internally but have real-time examples vis-à-vis the couple's interaction in the consulting room. Marital therapy typically moves back and forth between a recounting of incidents of the week, a description of how they relate to each partner's internal world, and a working through of moment to moment feelings and behavior in the therapy session.

Concluding Thoughts

The task of therapy is to transform. By using information derived from the formulation (character structure, implicit levels of functioning, central fantasies), in a safe atmosphere, the patient is fortified to undertake the rigorous and frightening work of understanding her internal world, and the equally challenging quest to make changes. Transformation is neither easy nor particularly welcome, in the beginning to be sure, but throughout the treatment. Individuals have fashioned lives that while filled with compromises that are less than satisfying, still offer a sense of safety and familiarity. We are asking a lot of our patients to give up the tried and true for the novel and unknown. Each member of the therapeutic duo has a lot on the line. To open oneself up to the possibility of raw and unprotected emotional interchange takes considerable courage, a marked contrast to those who find that those in therapy as "weak" and/or "dependent."

One transformation that occurs is that the nature of the therapeutic conversation becomes altered. The tone of sessions is more contemplative and more emotionally vibrant. Conversation moves smoothly from topic to topic; from outside to inside; from the patient's external life to the therapeutic relationship. The patient feels less afraid to bring difficult topics up; as does the therapist, as he feels more comfortable with his own sense of safety and that of the patient. This is not to say that hard times don't occur. But when they do, the pair have more tools on hand to deal with conflict. This all generalizes to the outside where conflicts that previously seemed insurmountable are handled with ease and confidence. The patient becomes an expert on his/her own personality, and this expertise creates a capability in facing and resolving conflict.

Note

1. See Hooberman (2002, 2007) for more discussion on this topic.

CHAPTER EIGHT

Forgiving, Forgetting, and Moving On

Reconciliation

The South African Truth and Reconciliation Commission was instituted in order for the country to obtain facts of human rights violations, grant amnesty when appropriate and establish a venue for victims and perpetrators to give testimony regarding their experiences during Apartheid.[1] The aim was not to punish but to give as full an airing of possible grievances and abuses, and to offer opportunities for individuals affected to come to terms with horrific experiences.

Just as the Commission was charged with the task of helping the country to integrate disparate factions of citizenry that had been embroiled in terrible conflict, psychotherapy is similarly dedicated to integrating seemingly incompatible areas of conflict into one's psyche. Therapy is designed to find the "truth"—the truth of one's feelings toward self and others, of being able to, with clear eyes, view relationships past and present and to capture, as much as possible, realities and truths of past events, and then to integrate them into one's present-day psyche.

The process of accommodation or reconciliation occurs during the working through and termination phases of therapy, where the central themes become worked over from a variety of angles, where effort is expended to widen previously narrow perspectives and where the patient is assisted in coming to grips with disappointments in self and in life. In this process, conflict is not vanquished; rather it is placed in proper perspective, and reconciliation between fervent desire and reality of possibility occurs.

I now turn to my final task, to elucidate how the potentially pernicious effect of conflict can be profitably turned toward further growth and development.

Therapeutic Effects

All of the personality factors that I have discussed—differing levels of consciousness and memory, attachment and separation patterns, symptom formation, defenses, affect regulation, self-states, degrees and quality of guilt and shame, quality of relationships, anger regulation, sexual desire—are addressed in a comprehensive therapy. In the therapeutic process, the therapist first illuminates (formulates a picture of the character structure as related to presenting problem) and then provides interpretations that touch upon compromise formations, relationships inside and out of the consulting room and characteristic defenses. All of this activity is designed to diminish conflict, so that the individual no longer becomes undone by intense feelings but well provisioned to meet the demands of life.

Before I turn more specifically to how one can ultimately come to terms with conflict, I will first describe the effects of successful treatment on several variables important in conflict resolution.

Balance

A healthy person feels much more in balance; conflict while not eliminated does not cause one to unravel. Rather it may very well be viewed as an opportunity for further growth. I have suggested a favorable outcome of enactments; where those involved in altercations are able to talk meaningfully to each other, to empathize with each one's positions, and to fashion a compromise that is reasonably satisfying to each. But balance is not just interpersonal; it represents an ability to sort through conflicting desires, reality constraints and potential disappointments in order to make self-enhancing choices. Strong emotions are good and are to be encouraged. But it is best if emotions do not overwhelm. Rather that a person can experience strong desires yet find reasonable ways to have them satisfied, without creating either internal or external conflict. It is all a matter of finding satisfaction without symptom formation. This occurs when one knows and accepts the facets of his internal world, and of the forces that have made up one's character structure.

Collaboration and Cooperation

As one progresses through therapy, a collaborative and cooperative feel permeates. There is a sense that the two participants are on the same page and that consensus exists as to the process and goals of the therapy. This is not to say that conflict disappears, and in fact, feelings become very intense in the middle and later stages of therapy, but they become manageable as both participants are committed to each other and to their jointly agreed upon task. Outside of the consulting room the patient is less at odds with others. Interpersonal conflicts are not eliminated, but they do not undo the individual. Instead she is comfortable in her own point of view and is able to stand her ground; and if found to be off the mark in a conflict, she is able to face responsibility without shame or guilt. A reasonable compromise is at least attempted, even if one is not always possible to achieve. In these instances, sadomasochistic dynamics that carry gratification through hostility don't hold the same allure as in the past. Rather the person takes pleasure in using her mind to solve problems without undue turmoil. Emotional upset is not valued; having good relationships with others is.

Because the individual is in balance, she doesn't require that others adhere to her needs. She respects the needs of others, and she recognizes and appreciates that her point of view is subjective, and not a truth. Within conflictual situations she works to find adequate solutions for all involved, and this cooperative feeling permeates, such that she can be cooperative and not antagonistic to her own needs and desires.

Empathy, Subjectivity, and Compromise

An ability to gain some measure of objectivity in the midst of personal and/or interpersonal achievement is a considerable achievement. Ironically, this is achieved when the patient can be empathic with self and others and can come to appreciate each person's subjectivity, their idiosyncratic points of view. When this is accomplished, one can move beyond insistence on any particular point of view toward recognizing that perception is guided by desire, and that everyone is approaching situations with some self-interest guiding their positions.

In soccer and other sports, we use referees to maintain fairness. In life we often are left to our own devices to figure out fair solutions to conflicts. Compromise should not mean "giving in." Rather compromise works best when a creative solution is found that is acceptable to all parties; that a new solution is found that, at least partially, meets the need of the parties involved.

Luke and Marie have faced numerous difficulties in conflict-laden situations. The bitterness engendered by their inability to fashion a compromise in the number of children to have is the most prominent example. But, as they asked me in the beginning of the treatment, "How do we move on from here?" One aspect of moving on is in gaining in the ability to compromise. For Luke and Marie, the notion of compromise is troublesome since each tends to feel that they are being forced to "give in." Pointing out that their typical attitudes toward conflict arise from family patterns is helpful, but it is also essential that each understand the "downstairs" reasons for the intensity of their desire. For Marie this means that finding a creative "third" solution does not necessarily represent humiliating failure or abuse, akin to her early relationships with her parents. Also it is important that she comprehends that her present desire, if not satisfied, does not mean that she was shamefully "wrong," only that it is crucial to take her husband's point of view into consideration. And, it is essential that she become cognizant of hidden sexual and aggressive wishes that have become linked with other seemingly more acceptable desires (like having more children) that fuel anxiety and shame. Luke has many of the same concerns, with the added consideration that he feels that when he "gives in" it represents an assault on his masculinity. Having empathy with self and others opens up the possibility of dialogue and compromise, in the best sense of the term.

Coping

Another conflict reduction goal is to achieve the ability to cope with adverse events. Having a stronger ego enables an individual to face conflicts with confidence, instead of the previous awkwardness and discomfort. It is quite common for patients to surprisingly notice that they are surmounting challenges that previously were felt to be out of the realm of possibility. The best changes are the ones that occur automatically, without consideration or willful effort. These represent changes at the implicit level of functioning, the place in the personality where the day-to-day work of living occurs. As one would expect from points I made earlier, the various levels of consciousness work in tandem. In other words, the entire psychic apparatus becomes positively altered, and situations that may have evoked tension and anxiety in the past are dealt with equanimity in the newfound level of psychic health.

In the past, Marie would become very upset when she was at odds with someone else. She would find herself ruminating with anger, anxious over potential conflict. As she now has a greater handle on the reasons for her tendency to become emotionally overwrought, she has more psychic room to consider options in problematic situations. Rather than returning to the automatic sense of somehow always being in the wrong (or always in the right with Luke), she has time and space to consider her responsibility within conflict without assigning undue blame to herself or to others. Now the default is not self-blame but is a wider consideration of causes and potential solutions—a change in her implicit level of functioning.

We do not expect that a person will be able to always maintain a sense of calm in all situations, in fact that would be inappropriate in cases when strong emotions are called for. But in general, it is hoped that a patient can achieve a sense of mastery over her internal world, such that when matters become intense, she can use her ego functions to make the best and not worst of a bad situation.

Complexity

One of the benefits that I have so enjoyed from my own personal therapy has been the ability to see and appreciate the complexity of my own mind. Therapy opens one's mind to new possibilities. And rather than being trapped in a narrow conception of how one ought to be and to think, a person with a successful therapy can take delight in considering choices and possibilities. Novice patients are surprised when I suggest that therapy, while very difficult and painful, can also be enjoyable. The relationship between patient and therapist is often one of the most meaningful ones in a person's life, and offers great and pleasurable possibilities for growth. It can bring great joy to peer into one's own mind, to appreciate its complexity, to be forever curious over its workings and to marvel at its ingenuity, for good and ill. And to participate in a process with a caring and expert navigator of waters that have seemed too treacherous and deep is not only curative in and of itself, but is an experience unlike any other. The complexity of the therapeutic process, where patient and therapist together travel the roads of love and hate, of desire and restraint, of fantasy and reality and of wishes for both regression and for maturity increases the capacity for holding contradictory desires in mind simultaneously. And being able to process matters of complexity is not only interesting but offers more opportunity to find effective solutions to conflict.

Winnicott once observed that even those with an antisocial bent still have hope, as they are still trying to obtain something from others, rather than falling into a chasm of despair. Not that I am suggesting that criminality is a good outcome but it is important to remember that every symptom, even criminality, represents the patient's perceived best chance for satisfaction and safety. In this regard, the adaptive mind is impressive in being able to fashion modes of gaining satisfaction even in the most adverse of situations. The often brilliant successes of compromise formations, although they can be ultimately detrimental, are, in a sense, accomplishments of mind over trauma, of rebellion over oppression and of freedom of thought over repression. That is why a therapist is best served to stand in respectful fascination over his patient's compromise formations. They represent considerable achievements. This attitude of viewing patients as using their minds to figure out the best solution that seems possible conveys respect for the complexity of each patient's mind, even if these compromise formations need to be set aside for others that are both healthier and more fulfilling.

Hope

No one would come into therapy if they didn't have some hope that they could be helped. Yet, once we get into the midst of the work, we find that hope may be in short supply, as the patient has had multiple experiences of desires thwarted and forbidden, and needs painfully denied. We also remember that the adaptive solutions achieved are felt to be the best choices available to the patient, and deliver some satisfaction, even if in the midst of pain. These compromise solutions are the patient's perceived best chance for some satisfaction or sense of safety, and they might very well represent a bulwark against despair. So even if one "hopes" matters can change, the underlying "hope" may be for the world and not the individual to change, and for omnipotent desires to become satisfied.

Akhtar (1996) makes the point that "someday and if only fantasies" represent intense wishes that the future will solve all ills, and that if the past could be rewritten, disappointments would disappear. Cooper (2004) writes of "pathological hope," an attempt to deny loss and is a fantasy of the reemergence of the omnipotent mother of the individual's early life (Akhtar, 1996). For the more disturbed, pathological hope is tenacious, but can be quite stubborn even in those with healthier constitutions. Some losses are difficult to process since they represent more than solely a loss of a relationship; they might represent a deeply held tie to an early attachment figure—one whom the patient feels he cannot live without. Or, accepting loss might open the person to feelings of guilt over the loved one's demise. Even more, loss may mean failure, or affects that feel too painful to manage.

Successful therapy leaves one with realistic hope, and confidence in one's ability to process disappointment without undue self or other blame, and confidence that the challenges of life can be dealt with effectively. This confidence is based upon a realistic appraisal of possibilities in life and in self, and a surrender of omnipotent wishes for the impossible.

Guilt and Shame

A successful therapy will result in a reduction in shame and guilt responses. The individual can detach present-day experiences from past events, allowing a more clear-headed assessment of misdeeds. Shame, although a ubiquitous human emotion, does not have much of a place in healthy psychology. First, it is hoped that one will figure out a way to avoid shame-inducing situations and, second, that behavior, thoughts or feelings that were previously felt as being shameful can be processed in a more empathic fashion.

Guilt can never be, and never should be eliminated from the psyche. Anxiety or guilt over contemplated misbehavior helps to keep us on the straight and narrow. And unconscious guilt is always going to be with us, as internal conflicts over competing desires and between desire and the forbidden never completely disappear. Yet, excessive and destructive guilt can and should be reduced through therapy. A healthy person doesn't need to agonize over whether or not to do something that might be out of character. Instead he knows automatically that a given behavior will violate his standards, and the temptation to transgress is minimal or even nonexistent. Guilty feelings previously linked with past fantasies or actions are now decoupled and reframed.

The individual acts in the present, meeting his needs without trampling on those of others. When he does do something that feels "wrong," he is able to understand his underlying motivations and to take actions to redress the wrong, either by speaking with the wronged party or by furthering self-exploration in order to gain understanding of his own psychological conflicts. From this perspective, most unhappy situations are not viewed as being calamities (see below) with guilt and/or shame associated, but with the recognition that disappointment is a natural aspect of the human condition. Disappointment then means that desires are not either bad or good (and neither shameful or guilt-ridden), but are again an aspect of being human. As such, it is not so crucial that specific desires are satisfied. Instead more interesting and satisfying alternatives may emerge when the burden that shame or guilt entails falls away.

When this transpires, as guilt and/or shame become less major motivating forces, internal and external conflict diminish. As with most archaically developed structures, aspects of the problematic features of these affects do not completely recede, but they are much less prominent.

Upstairs-Downstairs

The unconscious is not to be viewed as an ancient archeological tomb, with artifacts scattered about gathering dust. Rather, we are best served by thinking of a dynamic unconscious, a place where memories, feelings and thoughts exist not only from the distant past, but also move from the conscious mind to the unconscious, as defenses operate to protect the ego from pain. In this regard we can think of the "past unconscious" and the "present unconscious" (Sandler and Sandler, 1984). The work of therapy is designed, in regards to the past unconscious, to assist the patient to recover memories of specific events, feelings, thoughts and fantasies from the past as long as we accept the caveat that recall is not veridical but is distorted by an ego weakened by trauma, by the child's ability to process events, by subjectivity and by defensive maneuvers.

The therapeutic work is also aimed at assisting the patient in recognizing how contemporary events, feelings, thoughts and fantasies are placed in the present unconscious via defense operations. In this the patient doesn't only gain access to hidden aspects of the psyche but of characteristic methods of defense. In combining emphasis on both past and present unconscious, one gains greater understanding of the workings of the mind and attains a deeper knowledge of fantasies and events that have created his unique character. And this results in a more articulated sense of what drives him toward his choices and his conflicts. The patient is then able to forestall unfortunate decisions; he is able to craft new and creative solutions to old conflicts (both personal and interpersonal) and feels much less anxious and/or depressed.

The unconscious is not something that we ever even aspire to reduce; it is a source of neverending nutriment for the psychic soul. Rather we work toward diminishing its pernicious motivating forces, and to be able to use its power toward more beneficial means of conflict reduction. For instance, Maggie is now less driven by her need for order and control by being more in balance between "upstairs" and "downstairs." Len is moving toward being able to find more equilibrium in his life as he becomes more in touch with unconscious memories and painful affects. Marie's relationship with her husband is much improved as she sees how she is playing out her past identifications within her present-day marriage. Patients are best served by working toward this coherence between past and present.

Discharge

In the first chapter I wrote of the unfortunate propensity that some have to seek emotional discharge when facing conflict rather than seeking more thoughtful and considered actions. Len was this way of course, seeking out food to discharge feelings instead of using his mind to find effective solutions. He was neither mindful nor reflective, at least in the beginning of therapy. As we went on, though, his relationship (attachment) with me helped him to internalize more benign object representations leading toward a greater sense of safety. My interpretive work also was helpful in providing an intellectual foundation for an understanding of that which was previously bewildering. I demonstrated that talking and thinking were effective conflict resolution tools. He began to take more pleasure in our minds, and we enjoyed our sessions considerably more. We liked each other, which provided motivation for us to work together to companionably hash out painful memories and feelings. As the therapy progressed, he became more empathic with himself and others, and this was very much seen in his relationship with his children, where he was able to use reason and understanding instead of threat and intimidation when dealing with conflict. He also never realized how often he had evaded the truth in discussing difficult matters with those in and outside of his family and I helped him to understand that his mendaciousness was detrimental to his and others' well being. All of this work assisted him in being more able to talk more openly not just with me, but with others as well. Finding a more effective path toward conflict resolution, he needed to turn to affective discharge less often.

This was a similar process with Joyce. She and I came to understand that her wish to discharge affects represented several different needs and conflicts. Forbidden and denied (from her sterile marriage and from her character structure) from directly receiving sexual pleasure, Joyce knew no other way of gaining gratification except by the family model of sadomasochism. Better than nothing as it might be, my interpretation of this inadequate solution helped her to explore other possibilities. The therapy provided a venue for her sexual needs to be expressed transferentially, and we were able to examine her desires in a more direct way. Our positive feelings toward each other were curative in and of themselves. Feeling more secure in her attachment to me, she felt safer in exploring and examining her mind, opening up the possibilities of feeling more and feeling more intensely.

From this Joyce was able to speak more directly and honestly with her husband about her frustrations, and conflicts at work that had been felt as being overwhelming were now able to be confronted much more comfortably. Her ego was able to tolerate both frustrations and conflicts, and she was able to use her mind more productively to find effective solutions and, like Len, to reduce the need for affective discharge.

Regret—"If Only I Had a Time Machine"

Attaining a level of comfortable regret is not easy, to be sure. I have thought that the persistent desire to fashion a time machine reflects not only curiosity about past and future but also a fantasy of going back in time to undo either one's own actions or those of someone else; a wish to escape regret when regret feels beyond the capability to process reasonably. Cooper (2004) writes of what he refers to as "infinite regret," whereby an individual tenaciously holds onto the cruelty of fate, as a defense against deeply felt loss. Akhtar (1996) points out that "someday and if only fantasies" serve to protect from the challenge of confronting disappointments and failures.

Those who find regret beyond their ability to tolerate feel this way because the action regretted cannot be psychologically "placed" within the psyche. Actions that evoke too much regret may represent hidden (downstairs) memories or fantasies associated with past reproachful actions or wishes, often when these activities have become imbued with a sense of being forbidden not only from wrongdoing but from the then child's limited ability to properly assess right from wrong. Or, one's ability to process regret is overly threatened by a too-intense sense of failure, i.e., a blow to one's self-esteem—a narcissistic failure. Or, an individual may have done something he or she considers reprehensible and is not able to place those actions or others associated with them into a context that feels palatable.

A person who has experienced a more favorable upbringing is able to put regret and disappointment into perspective, not falling into the chasm of "if only" or neverending wishes for actions to be undone. Of course many who seek out psychotherapeutic assistance are trapped in "eternal regret" and cannot find ways to be freed. The process of therapy is designed to put regret in perspective, to help the patient to understand that past behavior cannot be undone, but that achieving an understanding of reasons for actions (in context of character and circumstance) can lead to gradual accommodation to past disappointments.

While in the past Marie was enraged over the impossibility of having more children (eternal regret) and of the betrayal of her husband, she is now filled with regret and remorse over her actions toward him. She now understands her husband was "steamrolled" when he objected to her notion of the number of children they were to have. In fact, she sometimes shakes her head in wonderment of her prior wishes as she enjoys the relative amount of free time she has now that her children are in school.

Her motivations can now be placed more in context, freeing her from the pain of intense regret. The driven quality of her desire to have six children reflects at least three issues: a powerful need to be loved, a wish to see herself as a procreator, not as one with strong sexual needs, and, finally, to perceive herself as someone who is self-sacrificial. Marie wanted to have scads of children as protection over her internal sense of badness. The strength of her desire matched the strength of her fear of negative self-representations. The understanding about her dynamics relieves the burden of regret. But what about her regret regarding her relationship with her husband?

Marie has attained the ability to speak more directly and honestly to her husband, and to feel empathic to each of their positions. From her experience in speaking with me over painful matters (including feelings in the consulting room), Marie is no longer as afraid of being emotional and vulnerable. She can also empathize with how her husband's upbringing (his internalizations) contributed to the "perfect storm" of their discontent. She knows that he is not without responsibility for their problems; his intransigence over his work schedule, his insecurities about being competent at work and his fear of vulnerability contributed to him consciously valuing work over family and contributed to them leading parallel lives. Their newfound ability to discuss their feelings has contributed to their internal and external lives being much more in balance and in perspective.

What about their disappointment? Those who come riven with internal and external conflict often have a lot riding on denying disappointment, as disappointment may carry the implication that the patient has abysmally failed in some cherished activity. But disappointment, in and of itself, is a normal aspect of life. It only becomes problematic when it becomes associated with extreme negative self-evaluations or reminds of past untenable disappointments. With the help of a therapist, a patient can come to put frustration and negative outcomes into a larger perspective, as part of a picture of life and character. Instead of being enraged at Luke, or at herself, Marie can now process her discomfort into disappointment. She can put her and Luke's behavior in context of their individual character structure and understand that their conflicts have emerged from the collisions of their psyche.

Regret and disappointment can become reified into ongoing internal and external tirades, or one can mobilize interior resources and move beyond to more creative solutions. I saw one couple in marital treatment where the husband had acknowledged an affair. His wife was understandably hurt and enraged; the husband was seemingly guilt-ridden and remorseful. But they moved no further. The wife continually berated her husband for his myriad "faults"; her husband castigated himself for his shortcomings and bad behavior, but in a fashion that appeared more gratifying than self-revelatory. Withstanding any therapeutic suggestions, neither could move beyond their sadomasochistic "death" grip to achieve deeper understanding of their dynamics. They left me frustrated and disappointed. I later heard from two other therapists whom had taken on their case, both who felt frustrated with the cemented positions of the couple.

There is another aspect of regret. That is when patients view past or future actions as being unquestioned catastrophes or calamities. As Len ponders whether to stay married to a woman for whom he feels little desire, he feels frozen in his choices. Being alone feels too risky. What if he never finds someone else? He also fears that his children will suffer too much if he's not always home. Yet remaining married seems untenable, as he feels that he is psychically dying from the dreariness of the union. We discuss these matters from myriad angles. We agree that every one of the issues that he raises are serious ones, and not to be lightly dismissed. Yet the notion that any choice will be calamitous must be examined further. It is our sense that he is associating past with present; that his past upbringing with a dissociated mother and an abusive father causes him to fear that his children's experience will match that of his own should he divorce, despite knowing that he and his wife are far more suitable parents.

Len fears leaving his marriage will result in him feeling too alone. He knows all too much about being alone. His mother's inability to properly and consistently attend to him created a firestorm of fear of abandonment. This impacted his marital choice, as he seemed to have married the first woman with whom he could form an attachment and didn't give himself the opportunity to find someone more suitable. Further he doesn't want his children to view him like he did his father, equating divorce with cruel abandonment. All of this discussion is helpful but only to a point. Our work needs to become more specific (moving from chapter titles to text) in order to help him find more specific feelings in the present and memories of the past in order to free himself from his quandary. Rather than making a precipitous decision, or of not making any decision, I suggest that he might want to put off a divorce decision for a bit as we continue to work together to get more access to hidden material. Meanwhile he and his wife might find it valuable to see another marriage counselor to address their issues in a straightforward manner and assist them in deciding whether staying married is in each of their best interest. By including his wife in the decision-making process, he then doesn't need to carry the burden by himself. To me this seemed like a reasonable way to work through the conflict; to respect his fears of "eternal regret" and to offer potential therapeutic solutions to enable him to make better and more reasoned decisions, and that potentially place he and his wife as collaborators, and not as antagonists.

Forgetting, Forgiving, and Moving On

Throughout this work I have described how therapists come to understand their patients, and then based on that understanding fashion interventions to lessen the deleterious effects of conflict. I have discussed at length the ways in which individuals struggle to accommodate conflict-laden feelings into their psyches, sometimes with more success, and often times with less. When all is said and done, those embroiled in conflict, whether within the self, or with others in the world, must make decisions as to how to handle that conflict—to forget, to forgive, and/or how to move on?

Forgetting

We forget in a variety of ways. We can consider any symptom as a form of forgetting, since the symptom represents the individual's "choice" as to how to put awareness of some aspect of life out of conscious consideration. Similarly, discharge through overt physical action or through compulsive behaviors (substance abuse, eating disorders, and other forms of acting out) is designed to enable the individual to not think (to forget) about disturbing matters.

I'm not a fan of forgetting, even though I too wish that some painful events and feelings could be wiped off the face of my psyche. Pushing feelings, memories and thoughts out of awareness may save the day in an immediate sense as an individual in a painful psychic situation must do something, and defensive denial may seem to be the best option. But in the long run, forgetting only substitutes symptom for temporary pain relief, often leading toward more and not less conflict.

Forgetting can seem like a viable option in dealing with conflict, both internal and within relationships. Yet we don't really forget, we repress, we deny, we disavow; we do what we can to make ourselves unaware of unpleasant realities. Just as South Africa has sought, at least by proclamation, to encourage truth telling and recollection (though I'm not naïve enough to believe that this process is not incredibly fraught), therapy is effective to the degree that truth, and that includes finding the truth of the past, is held as an ideal. Of course, we know that subjectivity and inadequacies of memory never really render an absolute "truth." But in the consulting room, we aim to develop a relationship that is built on truth and on remembering. In fact the endeavor is aimed toward capturing as many memories in the three memory systems I have designated (atmospheric, implicit and explicit). Remembering does not solely refer to the distant past. It also refers to recollecting that which just transpired, or to a thought that ran through one's mind the day before, painful experiences of mind that might offer the seduction of forgetting.

In remembering, the narrative becomes more and more complete and complex. Gaps understanding diminish and the patient is not prone to act out of the wish to not remember. Instead, knowledge is craved; history is cherished. Therapy takes courage, and it is the ability to let one know "truth" and to allow as full as possible access to memory that challenges one's bravery, and when faced, this challenge yields the best results toward working through conflict thoroughly and more effectively.

Len was a fervent advocate of forgetting. For instance, he and I had established that he treated complex thoughts like enemies; he never met any that he liked and did whatever he could to vanquish them from existence. He had several other weapons in his arsenal of psychic distraction. One of course was his eating; another was his sleepy yawning during sessions, and another was the aforementioned aversion to thought, and still another was his procrastination. The severity of symptoms indicates the severity of the trauma, and we had ample evidence of severity. And we were quite sure that his sparse memory of abuse was just the tip of the iceberg.

We can see that his symptoms were not only consequences of the traumas but also contained within them memories of the events. His reluctance to think represented his fear of thinking about specific traumatic memories; his sleepiness was designed also to lull our minds to sleep in order to not allow forgotten events in the past and of the present into the room (and represented a memory of his noninteractive bedtime rituals with mother), and he overate both to soothe but also to distract him from "remembering" matters that made him anxious. His procrastination again indicated a reluctance to be assertive, passivity in the present, and a suggestion of passive helplessness in the past. Being stuck in inaction also reflects anxiety about knowing unconcious desires.

Over time as he felt safer with me, he was able to use his mind more productively—to reflect upon himself and his actions. As his mind was more engaged, he no longer felt quite the need to use somnolence as a defense. His overeating, as it is with most people, was more intractable. However, he was able to begin to consider what he might be thinking about, or even not thinking about, when he felt the urge to overindulge. He started remembering incidents of sexual overstimulation but the specifics still were vague. Was it his thirteen-year-old aroused self in the bathtub with his three-year-old brother, or was it his aroused father with him? Dreams were remembered more frequently and again pointed toward early overstimulation. Not only the content could be remarked upon; it was important that now he was *remembering* his dreams, and not *forgetting* his thoughts and associations.

Gradually he is able to remember more, certainly more about present-day thoughts and feelings, and gradually and fitfully more about events in the past. The fear of remembering is so great that the progress is slow, but slow is okay, as we must respect the patient's need to not become overwhelmed.

The Wish to Forget

We also strive to forget in more conscious ways when we tell ourselves not to think about something that is bothersome, or that it's not worth being upset at such a small matter, and other such minimizations. Or, in relationships, injured parties are encouraged to brush aside their feelings, to live for the moment, to "forget" about their pain, or to ignore or rationalize bad behavior or betrayal. Those prone to these disinclinations to think also tend to unconsciously remove painful thoughts and feelings, as we know that defense, as an aspect of character structure, is likely to remain constant throughout levels of personality. The defenses that a particular patient is prone to use are often those found within the family of origin. Those who tend toward the practice of consciously being fond of pushing matters out of awareness are "speaking" the language of the family.

Many patients come to therapy questioning the wisdom of delving into painful matters. Maggie would often say to me, "I just want to put this behind me and move on." "This" would refer to any conflict that she felt potentially overwhelmed by, such as becoming aware of paternal sexual abuse. Even though I understood that this desire derived from extreme fear, I also knew (as did she eventually) that our best option was to continue to work toward greater understanding, and the recapture of memories repressed by trauma.

Other patients resist intensive therapeutic work, feeling that the bargain of not remembering, and not thinking is a good one, convinced that the option of thinking and feeling about matters that are frightening, seem more likely to open Pandora's Box, than the door to greater satisfaction in life. The process of therapy is designed to promote a sense of safety to enable individuals to face their anxieties, and to remember where they came from and to reclaim desire and hope.

As I have said, individuals are often encouraged or encourage themselves to "forget" about their own or other transgressions. This is seen often in relationships where those embroiled in conflict either consciously or implicitly agree to "forget" about aspects of a conflict. But the issues that are conflict-laden aren't really forgotten and will likely impact the relationship in ways both subtle and large. I am not suggesting that every unpleasant feeling should be expressed, or that every conflict needs to be discussed, either briefly or to death. But we need to keep in our awareness the fact of the conflict, its effect on us, and on the relationship.

Negative Hallucination

One aspect of "forgetting" is "forgetting" that which is right in front of one's face. This can be thought of as a negative hallucination. A patient was standing in front of me in a checkout lane at a grocery store. He looked directly at me, and I at him, and being sensitive to privacy concerns, I only smiled slightly. In the next session he made no reference to seeing me. I brought it up, and he was perplexed, having no memory of having seen me. Because of his already known propensity to dissociation, he had no difficulty in feeling at home with the situation I described. We came to understand that feelings of closeness and desire engendered by "seeing" me in a setting outside of the office was too much for him to process, resulting in a lacunae in his perception. We never did establish a recollection of the incident but the discussion was fruitful in identifying a characteristic defense against his very strong feelings in the present. If one cannot process or remember that which is occurring in the moment, one is at the mercy of the unconscious. The more one is able to remain cognizant of internal and external actions, one can be better able to confront conflict and to find effective maneuvers.

"I Can't Forget but I Can't Remember"

Maggie made this observation as she struggled to remember significant events in her childhood, notably whether her father had sexual contact with her. This is also an implicit acknowledgment that her symptoms are an indication that events that are not remembered are having a significant deleterious effect on her life. In this regard she forgot appointments, mixed up names and places and ignored aspects about her close friends and relatives. She became too embroiled in others' lives; to us an indication that she had trouble setting proper boundaries, which we suspected, was a memory (identification) of her parents' violations and externalizations. Another indication of her tremendous need to put troubling thoughts and memories out of awareness occurred in the therapy. At one point she said clearly to me, "When my father had sex with me. . . ." And then later in the session when I referred to her utterance, told me she didn't remember saying that. As I mentioned before, her need to forget existed in all levels of consciousness. And while the unconscious wish was reflected by a defense against remembering it also interestingly enough was a derivative of a memory. At one point in the midst of us trying to capture memories about potential sexual contact with her father, after listening to a radio program where a participant remarked on something he forgot,

Maggie reported "hearing" a voice, saying, "Just forget about it; put it out of your mind." She indicated that it was her father's voice. The memory resides within the symptoms.

But not being able to forget or remember is the tragedy of trauma, especially with severe trauma. The events are so troubling that they cannot easily be remembered, yet they continue to exist in a fashion that torments the individual. We also know that trauma affects ego functioning, often rendering memory distorted resulting in even more confusion and distress. If we remember what I said about adaptive solutions and compromise formations, it is clear that symptoms seem more appealing than remembering frightening and potentially overwhelming memories. It is within the therapeutic caring relationship that the constituent parts of compromise formations can be carefully sorted through allowing the patient to gradually remember memories and fantasies that so greatly contribute to both personal and interpersonal conflict. The narrative process of therapy helps the patient plagued by memory lapses, as patient and therapist work together to fashion a picture that is sufficiently explanatory even if the impossible ideal of verdicality is not met.

Len's wife asked him, in exasperation (he was threatening to end the marriage out of his unhappiness), why he can't forget about everything hurtful that transpired between them, and the abuse he suffered in the past, and just move on in the future. He told her, poetically and passionately, that forgetting had been enormously destructive to him, and he thought to her as well, and that he craved a life of honesty and truth, including being as aware as possible of the events of his and their lives, even if painful. He didn't know where his therapeutic path would take him, but he felt it would lead toward fuller awareness of his and their lives together, in as full remembrance as possible. I certainly couldn't ask more from him.

Forgiving

> When you have done something unforgivable, I'll tell you exactly what to do. You forgive yourself.
>
> —*House of Games* (Mamet, 1987)

In David Mamet's fascinating study of deception, *House of Games*, the protagonist (a psychiatrist, no less) who has murdered an antagonist asks her mentor (another psychiatrist), how to go on after committing the "unforgivable." The response, "When you have done something unforgivable, I'll tell you exactly what to do. You forgive yourself," simplifies and blithely excuses complex matters of guilt and remorse. But it does bring forth front and center crucial questions. How can one go on after having committed an offense?

How can one maintain relationships once wronged? How does "forgiving" fit in to conflict resolution?

In Marie's words, "Back when three of my children were four or younger, I had a lot of trouble coping. One time I remember I was trying to get them to go somewhere and they were not cooperating. I just lost it! I was struggling with the older child in the bathroom and all of sudden I grabbed her; I don't know what happened, she ended up with a bump on her head from the floor. I couldn't believe that I did that to her. I am so ashamed." She goes on to tell me of another time in the library, one of her children was acting up, not minding and she was so embarrassed that she took him out to the car and slapped him. "How could I do this? I am so ashamed." She tells me that she was raised with obedience as the primary goal, and she had believed that children are supposed to immediately be agreeable and obedient. I reiterate that in her family obedience seemed to be considered of great value. From our work together, she now feels differently and has different coping strategies, recognizing the value of being supportive and kind. She knows that what she used to do was negative and counterproductive in that everyone ended up angry, hurt and confused. She and I have worked hard at exploring other avenues for expression of frustration (affect management), and this, along with understanding of her internal representations and compromise formations, enabled her to find new identifications (with me), which along with her newfound ability to think more openly assisted in altering her interior landscape.

We also know that she hasn't only been overly critical toward her children, but that she is unmercifully self-denigrating as well. As we discuss these matters, I explain to her that she was raised in an authoritarian model, and that while it is important for parents at times to be authoritative, it is questionable how much value resides in being authoritarian. Eventually, her children will model her newly cooperative and empathic attitudes, and it will remain to be seen what effect her earlier behavior will have on them. But the fact that she is being far more open and willing to talk instead of punish will go a long way toward mitigating the negative effects from her earlier behaviors. On a deeper, less accessible level, I know that part of our work together will investigate other secret "sins" that also motivated her acting harshly to her children, that she is afraid to bring to light, for fear of being crushed by guilt. Also, from a transference point of view Marie is implicitly telling me that she is fearful that I will be as condemning of her as she was of her children. Interpreting this relieves anxiety and opens up opportunity for her to delve more deeply, and to feel safer in the process.

How can I help Marie to move beyond her agony over her past behavior? Forgiveness is a difficult concept to approach. For one, like guilt it is an ambiguous term, with many different and sometimes vague meanings. Akhtar (2002) enumerates many of these. For one, he points out, and I agree, that enlisting forgiveness can be a facile attempt to wipe away bad behavior by expressing false remorse while self-righteously begging forgiveness.

Yet, Akhtar emphasizes the importance of forgiving. "Forgiving others for their hurtful actions and forgiving oneself for having caused pain to others are crucial to moving on in life and to opening oneself for new experiences. An inability or unwillingness to forgive keeps one tied to the past and impedes development" (206). Smith (2008) has a position that is a bit different. He questions whether therapists should focus on forgiveness as a special point of inquiry and suggests that an emphasis on forgiveness occurs because, "of the work of accepting the reality of the traumas we have suffered—and which we have caused others to suffer—is so difficult and so fraught with failure that we embrace the promise that forgiveness will heal our pain, rage and guilt. The leap of forgiveness is a solution that has become part of our psychic lives" (932). He goes on to suggest that the working through of "bad" behavior is no different than the working through of any psychic activity and does not require a unique therapeutic focus.

I agree with Akhtar that one should own up to misdeeds, and that one should seek out the aggrieved party and try to make some sort of amends. Apology is a crucial component toward moving on beyond conflict. And it is essential that the wronged party be able to put aside bitterness and resentment and to accept or forgive once an apology is sincerely offered. But to me the more important question within a conflict is to ascertain the underlying dynamics that motivated the behavior that one regrets. In this regard, I am proposing that a careful analysis of the factors that contributed to the actions in question is most important. By proffering easy forgiveness, one reduces complex matters to easy solutions. "I'm sorry" is helpful, but should be the result of thoughtful scrutiny and inquiry, not a facile sweep under the rug.

It is important for Marie to confront her misbehavior but it is ultimately much more important for us to find the reasons for her actions. Easy and quick apologies close the door to further discourse and further inquiry and do not open the necessary door to further understanding.

How one comes to terms with hurt, disappointment and anger or interpersonal conflict depends on the way in which internal representations process hurt, disappointment and anger. An individual has internalized conflict management techniques and these automatically come to the fore in the midst of intense dysphoria. I have demonstrated this with both Luke and Marie, who too often fall back onto the tried and true family patterns and languages that they share. Another testament to their similarities is that each finds the others' behavior to be reprehensible and worthy of outrage, instead of a quest for empathy and understanding. In the throes of the agonizing feeling of being wronged, the others' behavior feels unforgiveable and worthy of punishment (Luke's wish to "freeze out" Marie). Luke and Marie do not escape self-condemnation, of course, and are no kinder to themselves than they are to the other, holding onto both internal and external grievances with great fervor. To help them fashion more reasonable solutions requires an alteration of the aspects of their character structure, such that new possibilities of conceptualizing hurt can be found.

But this is no small order, as we have seen through numerous case examples. Individuals "prefer" to remain wedded to the familiar, as the familiar represents both family and hard-won compromise formations. Those embroiled in sadomasochistic relationships need help in seeing that this kind of gratification, although compelling, leads only to ultimate unhappiness and bad feelings. It is not enough to show patients that, though; a therapist needs to demonstrate alternative ways of processing conflict. The emotionally intense and yet stabilizing force of the therapeutic relationship fortifies patients to make the leap to new and more open ways of relating (the Novicks' and Fairbairn's conceptions of open vs. closed systems), and in the back and forward intense therapeutic relationship creates these new representations.

Another aspect of the process of coming to grips with pain and loss is the ability to mourn, both of possibilities never attained, and of the reality of the imperfection of relationships. We all have the tendency to form fantasies as to the perfection of ourselves, and of others whom we love. Gradually realizing that neither person meets that ideal is, first of all, profoundly disappointing, second of all, humbling, and, lastly, and I say this with great hope, liberating. It is liberating in the sense that holding others and us to this ideal of perfection puts too much pressure on each. And an untethering of self and others to this ideal deepens the relationship since it allows real feelings and events to become more meaningful and memorable.

We all tend to operate, in some degree at least, with qualities of dissociation. When I discuss "upstairs" and "downstairs," I am suggesting that we have more than one "self" acting, feeling and thinking in any given circumstance. This is why we find ourselves becoming undone by situations that on the surface seem to be not so threatening. But internally we find similarities between past and present, between conscious and unconscious, between implicit and explicit memories such that a stimulating event may surprisingly provoke hurt, anger and resentment. The process of therapy links past and present, conscious and unconscious, implicit and explicit such that the past and the not known do not hold such sway in conflict, and different selves (conscious and otherwise) are more in sync. My conception of character structure assists in illuminating the complexity of the psyche, and its component parts, and shows how access to these components can work toward reducing the deleterious effects of conflict, leading toward a more "forgiving" attitude toward self and other.

When we speak of forgiving, it is essential that patients not only come to understand self and other, but to often positively appreciate the very qualities that they have found to be lacking in self and other. This is an example of "reframing" that I referred to in chapter 6. Marie and Luke can come to not only understand the underpinnings of their conflict, but to appreciate their levels of intense passion for each other that partially impelled the impasses. This process can eventually turn hard and unforgiving attitudes to those of love, compassion and profound appreciation.

To forgive oneself or others in the present, one recognizes limitations of self and life and chooses to not continue to be embroiled in conflicts that arouse self-abnegating passions. Instead one understands the imperfection and vulnerability that exists within us all and prefers to stay on the positive side of interpreting behavior, leaving recrimination and blame behind.

The Unforgivable

There are some actions that are perpetrated that are unforgivable. As I mentioned in the last chapter, some individuals are so overwhelmed by abusive memories that they can't even contemplate recapturing memories let alone try to reframe the actions and, of course, behaviors exhibited by Nazis and others of that ilk, past and present, are so horrific as to be beyond any sense of forgiveness. But to the extent possible, it is important that those who have had atrocities committed upon them need to be able to process these traumas in a fashion that they do not continue to be victimized by the past, or to feel badly because they could not protect themselves or loved ones. The fantasy that one has failed to act properly in a traumatic situation is compelling since it replaces passivity with activity and protects against an awareness of the profound helplessness experienced in the original trauma. Yet it also keeps the trauma alive; feeding unconscious fantasies that trauma can be undone. In this process, one does not mourn, and the past forever continues its hold on the present.

Maggie was like this, forever blaming her nine-year-old self for being a normally "incompetent" nine years old when her brother died, forever imagining a different outcome if only she had been more capable. This was a compensatory fantasy designed to block out helplessness, memories of that awful event, and fury at her parents for their profound neglect. Her habit of expecting to be able to manage any untoward event in the present harkens to this and other traumas and serves to keep extremely painful feelings and memories at bay. She would "prefer" self-blame over agonizing feelings of helplessness. And let's not forget how her unconscious fantasy world, with extreme feelings of anger and desire with corresponding senses of danger and the forbidden, exerts its effect, again having her hold herself responsible for what she considered dark and dangerous feelings.

My patient, Claire, was sexually abused and eventually abandoned by her father. Because of these actions, she suffered extreme deprivations and psychological dysfunction. She is embittered greatly by her father and his behavior, and she expresses no desire to "forgive and to forget." She holds great animosity towards him. All of this sounds (and is) quite reasonable. Yet, the past continues to haunt her, causing confusion between love and sex. Because of early sexual overstimulation, many affects become sexualized. She has trouble feeling affection for me without importing impelling sexual desire, trying to turn a trauma into a triumph, helplessness into mastery. The goal for Claire is not to either forgive or to forget but to unshackle the past from the present, and like with Maggie to allow her to feel the powerlessness and helplessness she felt, and to move beyond that anxiety to a sense of greater safety and security.

While forgiveness is important in conflict, from my point of view, it is more important to put past behaviors in context of the person's life, to be empathic with self and other, and to not be plagued by never-ending guilt or wishes for revenge that can never be realized; nor can self injured by the trauma be made whole.

Moving On

I have described the limitations of forgetting, and of the complexities of forgiving. Now I turn to how I envision the best outcome from painful conflict. When patients first enter therapy they are limited in their ability to see alternatives to their customary modes of thinking, feeling and acting. Because of the immense power of the mind, most are afraid of their own psyche, preferring to remain oblivious to its operations. This creates rigidity and concreteness of thought and an immovable categorization of experience. That is, the algorithms that have been developed to comprehend the internal and external world have become relatively fixed, without mental agility and fluidity to gain from new experiences. Because of potential discomfort, novel activities, experiences, feelings or thoughts are stripped of interesting complexity and are simplified into already existing categories that are often both simplistic and devoid of color. Those diagnosed as "Borderline" are seen as having the tendency to view matters as either "black or white." It is not only the seriously disturbed that have this reductionist tendency. Under stress we all try to simplify and group experiences into categories, much like when people are labeled as either "liberal" or "conservative" as if those words adequately convey a person's defining qualities.

When Len felt stressed before therapy, he didn't contemplate the reasons for his distress; rather he dealt with his discomfort by dumping his feelings and potential thoughts into the "I'm stressed and therefore I overeat" container. He had very few options for satisfactory "placement" of his too-intense affects. Now with some years of therapy under his belt, he has more categories into which he can place and understand his dysphoria. Presently he can consider whether and how a given situation makes him feel sad, or reminds him of his experiences with his abusive father, or dissociative mother, and so on. He can recognize his discomfort before he overeats or dissociates, and even if he is not yet able to completely reduce his symptomatic behavior, he is developing a much wider sense of the meaning of his behaviors; and this in turn leads to a more nuanced and elaborated sense of self, as well as more reflective and contemplative thinking.

This is for me the essence of moving on, being able to expand one's psychic horizons, to be able to think more deeply about conflict, to understand one's own contribution, one's own internal dynamics, and to fashion a way of "placing" the conflict in the psyche in a fashion that leads toward creativity and away from stagnation. This is accomplished through a therapy that, for me at least, emphasizes understanding of character structure—on how underlying dynamics have contributed to conflict, and/or to an inability to process conflict in more comfortable fashion. From that understanding I have described various therapeutic activities that lead toward a more balanced psyche, one that is able to handle affects without undue disruption, that is competent and successful in relationships, that is able to compromise when called for, or stand one's ground when necessary.

I have also emphasized the importance of helping patients to develop a narrative that links past and present, that helps them to look back on their lives, and to weave experiences into a tapestry of complexity and meaning. A fuller appreciation that life is not capricious but is a consequence of not always consciously willful choices is centering to those who have felt that their life has been buffeted by forces beyond their ability to comprehend. Patients are able to see that consistency exists within their life choices and that this consistency comes from a fascinating amalgam of character and, of course since life is not always predicable, happenstance.

Finally to illustrate the manner in which individuals can move on after conflict, I will describe the changes made by Maggie and Luke and Marie (I have described Joyce's changes earlier in this chapter) through their therapies. All of their therapeutic work is still in process but I would like to elaborate on how each are moving beyond conflict into more satisfying psychic places.

Luke and Marie

Luke and Marie are alike in many ways. They resemble each other physically, have similar family dynamics and many of their internal struggles are, although not identical, certainly in the same ballpark. This is not surprising since our primary narcissism impels us to be attracted to those that are similar to us. It can also create problems since we also find others whose psychopathology also fits in with that which is familiar, and which fits in with our unconscious healthy needs.

From an educative point of view, I had instructed them on the work of therapy and described to them, from my formulation, how their family upbringing had established internal representations and general character structures that created internal and marital strife.

The initial turning point in the marital therapy occurred when Marie was able to hear from me (but not from her husband) that she had acted unreasonably in insisting on the size of the family. This helped them move toward more open discussion of their bitter feelings, and a wish for a better relationship. We continued to explore their family dynamics and indicated their contributions to both character structure and conflict. Moving beyond "chapter and title" we moved toward a textual analysis of their everyday relationships, looking closely at the in-the-moment pressures that contributed to their discord. After several months of work, with his marriage stabilized, Luke decided to withdraw from the therapy. It was my feeling that he felt threatened by the approaching vulnerability that continued treatment would expose. Nevertheless from reports from Marie, he continued to work on his contributions to their distress, although I still felt he needed more assistance in order to delve more deeply. Although I certainly wished he had continued, I also realize that as with most aspects of life, we often must settle for less than perfection, and I hope that one day he will return to therapy.

And Luke and Marie must come to grips with imperfection as well, both that of their own and of their partner. Like with many, Luke and Marie guard against debilitating feelings of anxiety by initially denying any contribution to their discord. It is only later in the therapy that they can look and come to accept their own contributions to their distress.

And this is part and parcel of the process of being able to move on beyond conflict, to recognize the underpinnings of their behavior, its consequences to their own functioning and to their relationships. Placing these behaviors, feelings and thoughts in context of character structure helps to reduce the compelling quality of one's need to punish self or other. An appreciation of one's unconscious also assists in this regard, as Marie, through more intensive therapy, moves toward understanding how her profound sense of fragility stems from early experiences, both remembered and forgotten. The retrieval of memory again leads toward clarity as to how and why she feels and behaves the way she does, why she pushes Luke away sexually. To allow her sexual needs to come to the fore frightens her, as shame has forced such desires underground. Being one of strong desires is a good quality, but being afraid of one's desires is a problem. And Marie was certainly afraid of them, "allowing" Luke to carry the weight of the desire, while she acted as the guardian of the "goodness" of sexual denial. This awareness provided a wider perspective, reduced her anxiety, lowered the level of tension in the home, and enabled her to move on beyond her and her husband's transgressions. Our continued relationship will provide a present-day venue for Marie to microscopically investigate feelings of forbidden desire and her defenses used to keep her ignorant, and it will assist in freeing herself from the constraints of guilt and shame.

I have emphasized empathy as a necessary component toward the reduction of conflict, and attaining empathy for Luke was an important step in her treatment. She described to me some cranky behavior on her children's part, then went on to describe Luke's behavior that seemed to me to be not that different from the children. With her children she was warm, loving and understanding. With her husband she was critical and condemning. I pointed this out to her, and she was taken aback. We discussed her need to push him away that we felt, at the least, represented a fear of vulnerability, and a projection onto him of what she perceived were her own shortcomings. This newfound empathy enabled her to become kinder to her husband, and he was grateful for that and began responding in kind. And of course, I needed to help her in becoming more empathic with herself, curious instead of critical and open to reframing and to new understandings.

It was not only empathy, though. I also emphasized two important behaviors in relationships. The first is elaborated communication. By this I mean a sharing of points of view, listening without condemnation and defensiveness (again an ideal not easily achieved), being empathic and sympathetic, appreciating a different point of view, and the nature of subjectivity. The second is that in a marriage, maintenance of the relationship is far more important than becoming embroiled in sadomasochistic satisfaction of anger and vengeance. Although this seems self-evident, Marie and Luke found it difficult to let their guards down and to allow a deeper and potentially more satisfying relationship to develop. Each had been hurt and shamed too much and too often. But stating what may be obvious was helpful to them, as they had never put it into words before. Work remains to be done, and yet I am very confident that we will be able to achieve considerable progress. I also imagine and hope that I'll hear from Luke again some day.

But I do know that much has improved in their lives, individually and in their marriage. And they are now able to "place" their conflicts in context and in doing so are able to move beyond recrimination toward a relationship that is not without scars, but that is far deeper and more meaningful than before. They have not forgotten, have not exactly forgiven, but do appreciate the complexity of both of their psyches and of their relationship.

Maggie

Maggie is a victim of trauma, and as such has much she wishes she could forget. She finds "negative" feelings to be unsightly, associated with at times feces. She abhors messiness and imagines that I do as well. This projection causes her to keep much to herself as she defensively thinks to herself that her thoughts are "trivial" or "messy" or "dirty" even though I have strongly encouraged her to tell me everything on her mind, and she "knows" that I won't condemn.

Even though the therapeutic process shows demonstrated benefit, Maggie soon falls back upon her implicit assumption that her thoughts will likely lead us nowhere good. She has placed memories that feel both too painful and too shameful in psychic places that she wishes were inaccessible. Anxiety remains as a potent reinforcer in the illusion that denial will keep her safe while she remains "calm, cool and collected." This strategy has been found to be less than effective, and Maggie is gradually loosening her hold on her defenses and is willing to venture out more, internally, in the consulting room and socially, taking more a risk of exposure and potential shame. Despite having trepidations, these movements toward greater emotional interactions have been quite rewarding, a result of an expanded capacity to consider the reasons for her social isolation (condemnation if she has anything less than positive feelings toward others, shame over these feelings and perhaps most strongly, anxiety over being exploited, sexually and otherwise). All of this has been discussed and gone over at length, and some of the intensity of her fear has decreased, and she has more room in her psyche to contain nuanced relationships. On one hand, she can recognize the imperfections of self and others and not write others off immediately and, on the other hand, she allows herself to find self and others to have interesting attributes—these self same attributes that she has previously disavowed. Her blithe denial of her own perceptions of others' suitability has been a problem, as she is too quick to not be too judgmental, resulting in not being discerning at all. Increased flexibility and openness enables her to not only be able to process conflict, but has created a space for more pleasurable activities as well.

As Maggie remembers more, memories replace symptoms. Our relationship is strong and intense, and it is our bond that allows her to move toward recalling memories of events that were too overwhelming to be able to be processed by her young and unformed ego. The memory of sexual abuse is becoming clearer, and Maggie is able to place that abuse in context of her character structure, understanding how it affected her sense of self, her conscious and unconscious fears, her fantasies, her anxieties and her relationships. Conflict is understood within this, and Maggie feels steadier in her ability to face both her internal wishes and fears, and the conflict between wishing for relationships and her tremendous fear of betrayal.

When Maggie first sought out treatment she told me that her family background was "fine," having no conscious sense of the extreme privations she faced. It didn't take long, just scratching the surface so to speak, for her to see clearly, and yet not clearly, how disturbance ran rampant through her family. Over time, our process helped to remove the negative self-attributions to her circumstances. Instead of self-blame she too could see her life and her choices in context. No longer self-deprecating, Maggie understands, implicitly and explicitly, that she was a victim and not a perpetrator, and that it is possible for her not to continue to be victimized by experiences beyond her ability to affect.

Self-Determination

The more we are controlled by our unconscious world of unprocessed affects, fantasies and memories, the less control we have over our choices in life. In contrast, the more that we understand our interior landscape, the more able we are to make choices that guide our life in a fashion that is rewarding and pleasurable. In this regard, a person who is in healthy balance can make smooth and reasonably unconflicted decisions as to the rightness or wrongness of actions leading toward choices that are in one's best interests.

Trauma can never be undone; whether it reflects abuse, illness or extreme discord it will always have an effect. We hope to minimize the effect and to not continue to reify the trauma into a definition of life. Moving on requires a process of changing the algorithms, implicit levels of personality development, the working models of behavior, the operating systems and procedures that have guided and controlled our thoughts, feelings and behavior. More flexible and open operating systems can develop from the various therapeutic interventions that I have described.

I have never met anyone who, if we look under a veneer of certainty and confidence, is not, initially at least, afraid of her own mind. And this is why after being in this field for thirty-five years, I am not surprised by attacks on depth psychotherapy. But I cannot imagine how one can hope to affect profound changes in a patient's life without delving deeply into the more inaccessible reaches of the mind, into the areas in which the origins of conflict reside.

Altering the Nature of the Discourse

It is clear that I feel that the goal of psychotherapy is not to achieve a conquering or ridding one of myriad conflicts and "issues," but to be in greater psychic balance. Psychotherapy values thought over reckless action, so that it is hoped, for instance, that Joyce can learn to use her mind to solve problems, rather than act self-destructively, and that Marie and Luke can find a way to both understand themselves and each other better, and to talk about their disparate views without acting them out through hostility, in other words to *alter the nature of their discourse*, both externally and more importantly internally.

The internal dialogue or discourse is mostly not a real conversation. Rather it operates at the implicit nonverbal level, where the work of the psyche operates automatically. The procedures that the ego uses to maintain the business of moving through life smoothly usually function without conscious volition. In the best outcome one can hope for, wishes, choices, feelings, thoughts and behavior flow unimpeded without anxiety, indecision or blame or inhibition.

The therapeutic process is, in part, designed to help the patient to consider aspects of his or her internal life from a different perspective, which then alters the nature of the discourse, internally and by extension, with others. This widened perspective allows for thoughts, feelings and behaviors previously inhibited or deemed forbidden to come to the fore. As a patient progresses the nature of the dialogue between therapist and patient changes as well. A greater degree of intimacy occurs, ideas and feelings flow more easily; the process is collaborative, meaningful, satisfying and enjoyable—worthy goals for all relationships. The internal world is less fragmented. More "spaces" exist where conflictual matters can be placed. Conflict no longer overwhelms; the individual feels more reconciled with self, others and with life. Disappointments are accepted as inevitable, not necessarily as failures, and as opportunities for further growth.

And this is what we see in a healthier personality—the ability to consider wider points of view, to be open to new possibilities, to carry on the therapeutic process by oneself, and to allow newer and more exciting conversations, both internally and externally. And of course, to be able to face and work through conflict, and to move on beyond it, to meet new challenges and opportunities, often times never even imagined as desirable or possible.

Note

1. I am indebted to Murray Meisels, PhD, for his suggestion that the thesis of this book has similarities to South Africa's Truth and Reconciliation Commission.

References

Ainsworth, M., M. C. Blehar, E. Waters, and S. Wall. 1978. *Patterns of Attachment: A Psychological Study of the Strange Situation*. Hillsdale, NJ: Erlbaum.

Akhtar, S. 1996. "Someday . . ." and "if only . . ." fantasies: Pathological optimism and inordinate nostalgia as related forms of idealization. *Journal of the American Psychoanalytic Association* 44:723–53.

———. 2002. Forgiveness: Origins, dynamics, psychopathology and technical relevance. *Psychoanalytic Quarterly* 71:175–212.

Auerhahn, N., and D. Laub. 1998. The primal scene of atrocity: The dynamic interplay between knowledge and fantasy of the holocaust in children of survivors. *Psychoanalytic Psychology* 15:360–67.

Beebe, B., and F. Lachmann. 2005. *Infant Research and Adult Treatment: Co-Constructing Interactions*. Hillsdale, NJ: The Analytic Press.

Blatt, S. 2006. A fundamental polarity in psychoanalysis: Implications for personality development. *Psychoanalytic Psychology* 26:494–520.

Bollas, C. 1987. *The Shadow of the Object: Psychoanalysis of the Unthought Known*. New York: Columbia University Press.

Bowlby, J. 1969. *Attachment and Loss: Volume 1: Attachment*. London: The Hogarth Press and the Institute of Psychoanalysis.

Brenner, C. 1982. *The Mind in Conflict*. New York: International Universities Press.

Britton, R. 1995. Psychic reality and unconscious belief. *International Journal of Psychoanalysis* 76:19–24.

Bromberg, P. 2001. *Standing in the Spaces: Essays on Clinical Process, Trauma and Dissociation*. Hillsdale, NJ: The Analytic Press.

Busch, F. 1995. *The Ego at the Center of Clinical Technique*. Northvale, NJ: Jason Aronson.

Cooper, S. H. 2004. State of the hope: The new bad object in the therapeutic action of psychoanalysis. *Psychoanalytic Dialogues* 14:537–51.
Dapretto, M. 2006. Understanding emotions in others: Mirror neuron dysfunction in children with autism spectrum disorders. *Nature Neuroscience* 9:28–30.
Droga, J. T. 1997. Realities lost and found: Trauma, dissociation, and somatic memories in a survivor of childhood sexual abuse. *Psychoanalytic Inquiry* 17:173–91.
Erikson, E. 1950. *Childhood and Society*, 2nd ed. New York: Norton.
Fairbairn, W. D. 1952. *Psychoanalytic Study of the Personality*. London: Tavistock.
———. 1958. On the nature and aims of psychoanalytic treatment. *International Journal of Psychoanalysis* 39:374–85.
Fonagy, P. 1991. Thinking about thinking: Some clinical and theoretical considerations in treatment of a borderline patient. *International Journal of Psychoanalysis* 72:639–56.
Fonagy, P., and M. Target. 1996. Playing with reality: I. Theory of mind and the normal development of psychic reality. *International Journal of Psychoanalysis* 77:217–33.
Fraiberg, S., E. Adelson, and V. Shapiro. 1987. Ghosts in the nursery. In *Selected Writings of Selma Fraiberg*, ed. Louis Fraiberg. Columbus: Ohio State University Press.
Freud, S. 1900. The Interpretation of Dreams. *The Standard Edition of the Complete Psychological Works of Sigmund Freud*, vol. 4, ix–627.
———. 1912. Papers on Technique. *The Standard Edition of the Complete Psychological Works of Sigmund Freud*, vol. 12, Recommendations to Physicians Practicing Psychoanalysis, 109–20.
———. 1917. Mourning and melancholia. *Standard Edition* 14:239–58.
Fulghum, R. 1988. *All I Need to Know I Learned in Kindergarten*. New York: Ballantine.
Ghent, E. 1990. Masochism, submission and surrender: Masochism as a perversion of surrender. *Contemporary Psychoanalysis* 26:108–36.
Grey, P. 1994. *The Ego and the Analysis of Defense*. Northvale, NJ: Jason Aronson.
Herman, J. 1992. *Trauma and Recovery*. New York: Basic Books.
Hooberman, R. 2002. *Character Transformation through the Psychotherapeutic Relationship*. New York: Jason Aronson.
———. 2007. *Competing Theories of Interpretation: An Integrative Approach*. New York: Jason Aronson.
———. 2008. Roles of engagement: Commentary on paper by Richard Almond. *Psychoanalytic Inquiry* 18:95–103.
Kernberg, O. 1967. Borderline personality organization. *Journal of the American Psychoanalytic Organization* 15:641–85.
Killingmo, B. 1989. Conflict and deficit: Implications for technique. *International Journal of Psychoanalysis* 70:65–79.
Klein, D. 1998. *Organizing strands in the treatment of adolescents*. Paper given at the Michigan Psychoanalytic Council, East Lansing, MI.

Klein, M. 1946. Notes on some schizoid mechanisms. *International Journal of Psychoanalysis* 27:99–110.
Kohut, H. 1971. *The Analysis of Self*. New York: International Universities Press.
Krystal, H. 1988. *Integration and Self-Healing: Affect, Trauma, Alexithymia*. Hillsdale, NJ: The Analytic Press.
Lachmann, F. M., and J. Lichtenberg. 1992. Model scenes: Implications for psychoanalytic treatment. *Journal of the American Psychoanalytic Association* 40:117–37.
Langs, R. 1979. Interpretations in the bipersonal field. *Contemporary Psychoanalysis* 15:1–54.
Lichtenberg, J. 2005. *Craft and Spirit: A Guide to the Exploratory Psychotherapies*. Hillsdale, NJ: The Analytic Press.
Loewald, H. W. 1960. On the therapeutic action of psychoanalysis. *International Journal of Psychoanalysis* 41:16–33.
Luborsky, L. 1984. *Principles of Psychoanalytic Psychotherapy: A Manual for Supportive-Expressive Treatment*. New York: Basic Books.
Mahler, M. 1975. *The Psychological Birth of the Human Infant: Symbiosis and Individuation*. New York: Basic Books.
Main, M., and J. Solomon. 1986. Discovery of an insecure-disorganized/disoriented attachment pattern: Procedures, finding and implications for the classification of behavior. In *Affective Development in Infancy*, ed. T. B. Brazelton and M. Yogman, 95–124. Norwood, NJ: Ablex.
Mamet, D. 1987. *House of Games*.
McWilliams, N. 2003. The educative aspects of psychoanalysis. *Psychoanalytic Psychology* 20:245–60.
Miller, S. 1996. *Shame in Context*. Hillsdale, NJ: The Analytic Press.
Morrison, A. 1989. *Shame: The Underside of Narcissism*. Hillsdale, NJ: The Analytic Press.
Novick, J., and K. K. Novick. 2004. The superego and the two-system model. *Psychoanalytic Inquiry* 24:232–56.
Sandler, J. 1983. Reflections on some relations between psychoanalytic concepts and psychoanalytic practice. *International Journal of Psychoanalysis* 64:35–45.
Sandler, J., and A. Sandler. 1984. Interpretation: The past unconscious, the present unconscious, and the analysis of transference. *Psychoanalytic Inquiry* 4:367–99.
———. 1987. The past unconscious, the present unconscious, and the vicissitudes of guilt. *International Journal of Psychoanalysis* 68:331–41.
———. 1992. Psychoanalytic technique and theory of psychic change. *Bulletin of the Anna Freud Centre* 15:35–51.
Shengold, L. 1978. Kaspar Hauser and soul murder: A study of deprivation. *International Review of Psychoanalysis* 5:457–76.
Smith, H. F. 2008. Leaps of faith: Is forgiveness a useful concept? *International Journal of Psychoanalysis* 89:919–36.
Spence, D. 1982. *Narrative Truth and Historical Truth: Meaning and Interpretation in Psychoanalysis*. New York: Norton.

Stern, D. 1983. Unformulated experience—From familiar chaos to creative disorder. *Contemporary Psychoanalysis* 19:71–99.

Stern, D., L. Sander, J. Nahum, A. Harrison, K. Lyons-Ruth, A. Morgan, N. Bruschweilerstern, and E. Tronick. 1998. Non-interpretive mechanisms in psychoanalytic therapy: The "something more" than interpretation. *International Journal of Psychoanalysis* 79:903–21.

Tuch, R. H. 2007. Thinking with, and about, patients too scared to think: Can non-interpretive maneuvers stimulate reflective thought? *International Journal of Psychoanalysis* 88:91–111.

Van der Kolk, B. 1987. *Psychological Trauma*. New York: American Psychiatric Publishing.

Wallin, D. J. 2007. *Attachment in Psychotherapy*. New York: Guilford.

Weiss, J., and H. Sampson. 1986. *The Psychoanalytic Process*. New York: Guilford.

Index

accommodation, 121–22
adaptive mind, 51–52
addictive mind, 54–55
affects: healthy expression of, 76–77; management of, 75–76; of misdeeds, 66–71
affirmation, 100–102
Akhtar, S., 126, 130, 139
anger, 77–78
anxiety: addictive, 54–55; central, 39–41; versus control, 57
assessment, 95
associations, 26, 28–29
atmospheric memory, 12, 14–15
attachments: nature of, 71–75; types of, 72–73
attention, Freud on, 115
attribution errors, 11, 58
autonomy, 68
avoidant attachment, 72–73

balance, psychotherapy and, 122
Bowlby, J., 72
Brad (patient), 90–92

central fantasies, 39–41; and narrative development, 107
central themes, 41; and interpretation, 108
character structure, 7, 9–10; construction and, 37; development of, 15–22
child. *See* parent-child relationships
closed system, 46–49
collaboration, psychotherapy and, 123
complexity, psychotherapy and, 125–26
compromise, psychotherapy and, 123–24
conflict, ix–x, 1–5; closed system and, 49; and defenses, 84–85; definition of, 2; development of ability to deal with, 61–81; external versus internal, 10; forgiving and, 137–42; formation of, 25–42; intrapsychic, 78; moving on from, 142–44; reconciliation of, 121–22
constructions, 11–12, 36–37
control, 57–58
Cooper, S. H., 130

cooperation, psychotherapy and, 123
coping, psychotherapy and, 124–25
countertransference, 112–15; and nonconscious phenomena, 26–27; relation to transference, 114–15; and unconscious communication, 31–32
criticism, 65–66
curiosity, 65–66

defenses, 84–85; in action, 85–87; and anger and hostility, 77–78; and forgetting, 34; and motivation, 111
delicacy, in psychotherapy, 109
derivative, 26, 28
desire, 78–79; sexual, 79–80
development, 61–81
discharge, 3, 76–77; psychotherapy and, 128–29
discourse, internal, altering, 148–49
dissociation, 89–92; psychotherapy and, 140–41
doubt, shame and, 68
dreams, and nonconscious phenomena, 27–28

education, psychotherapy and, 105–7
effects, versus intention, 58–59
efficacy, 61–64
ego: partitioned, 83–92; strength of, 76
Emma (patient), 37–38
emotions. *See* affects
empathy, 97–99, 123–24
empty self, 88–89
enactments, 87
Erikson, E., 68
explicit (episodic) memories, 12–13
external conflict, 10

Fairbairn, W. D., 89
false self, 88–89
fantasy(ies), 37–39; central, 39–41, 107
father. *See* parent-child relationships
flexibility, mental, 45–49
Fonagy, Peter, 49–50
forgetting, 1, 33–34, 133–37; nonconscious, 34–36; wish for, 135–36
forgiving, 1, 137–42
formulation process, 15
Fraiberg, S., 10
free association, 28–29
Freud, Sigmund, 10, 27, 115
Fulghum, Robert, 55

guilt, 66–71; nature of, 69; psychotherapy and, 127

hallucination, negative, 136
helplessness, 57–58
hope, psychotherapy and, 126–27
hostility, 77–78
human development, 61–81

identity, versus character structure, 9
implicit memories, 12–14
incompetence, 61–64
individuation, 71–75
insecure attachment, 72
intention, versus effects, 58–59
interaction, in therapeutic relationship, 115–18
internal conflict, 10–11
internal discourse, altering, 148–49
interpretation, 27, 108–9; definition of, 108
interventions: indications for, hierarchy of, 108–9; therapeutic, 95–119
intrapsychic conflict, 78

James (patient): and countertransference, 31–32; and fantasy, 38; and guilt and shame, 69–71; and therapeutic relationship, 116–18
Joe (patient), 85

Joyce (patient): and anxiety, 55; and conflict, 2–3; and discharge, 76–77, 129

Ken (patient), 103–5
Kevin (patient), 56–57
Killingmo, B., 109
Klein, M., 58
Kohut, H., 100

Laura (patient), 111
Len (patient): and affect management, 75–76; and countertransference, 112–14; and criticism, 65–66; and discharge, 129; and educative aspect, 106–7; and forgetting, 134–35, 137; and meaning, 110; and mental flexibility, 46–51; and motivation, 111–12; and moving on, 143; and reframing, 102; and regret, 132
Lisa (patient), 53–54
Lois (patient), 97–99
Louise (patient), 64
Luke (patient), 16–19; and anger and hostility, 77–78; and compromise, 124; and conflict, 4; and constructions, 12; and forgiving, 140; and moving on, 144–46; and regret, 131; and sexual desire, 80

Maggie (patient): and association, 29; and central fantasy, 39–41; and defenses, 86; and derivative, 28; and enactments, 87; and forgiving, 141–42; and memory, 13–15, 32–33, 35–36, 136–37; and mind, 51–52; and moving on, 146–47; and observation, 99–100; and wish to forget, 135
Mamet, David, 137
Marie (patient), 19–22, 96–97; and anger and hostility, 77–78; and association, 29–30; and compromise, 124; and conflict, 3–4; and constructions, 12; and efficacy, 63–64; and forgiving, 138–40; and moving on, 144–46; and narrative development, 107; and regret, 130–31; and self-judging, 67; and self-states, 88; and sexual desire, 80
marital therapy, 118; guilt and shame and, 69–71. *See also* Luke; Marie
meaning, 109–10
meeting, moments of, 115–16
memory, 33–34; dangers in, 37; difficulties with, 136–37; and formulation, 15; and guilt and shame, 67; storage of, 34; types of, 12–15. *See also* forgetting
mentalizing, 90
mind: adaptive, 51–52; addictive, 54–55; complex, 61–81, 125–26; development of, 61–81; flexibility of, 45–49; partitioned, 83–92; and problem solving, 45–59; reflective function, 49–51; stuck, 55–57, 140
mirroring, 100–101
moments of meeting, 115–16
mother. *See* parent-child relationships
motivation, 110–12
mourning, 140
moving on, 142–44

Nancy (patient): and attribution error, 11; and memory, 12
narcissism, 55
narrative, development of, 107
negative hallucination, 136
nonconscious forgetting, 34–36
nonconscious phenomena, 26–33; psychotherapy and, 128
nonverbal communication, 26, 30–31

object, 10
object-representation, 11
observation, 99–100
open system, 46

paranoid position, 58, 109; and anger and hostility, 77
parent-child relationships: and attachment, 71–75; and character structure, 10, 15–22; and curiosity versus criticism, 65–66; and efficacy versus incompetence, 61–64; and guilt and shame, 66–71
pathological hope, 126
problem-solving mind, 45–59
procedural memory. *See* implicit memories
psyche, nature of, 9–23
psychotherapy, ix–x; and balance, 122; and collaboration and cooperation, 123; and complexity, 125–26; and compromise, 123–24; and coping, 124–25; and discharge, 128–29; educative aspect of, 105–7; and guilt and shame, 127; and hope, 126–27; interactive, 115–18; and nature of discourse, 148–49; and regret, 130–32; safety and, 103–5; and transformation, 112, 118–19; and unconscious, 128

Rachel (patient): and attachment, 73–76; and dreams, 27–28; and unconscious communication, 30–31
reconciliation, 121–49
reconstructions, 36–37
reflective function, 49–51
reframing, 102–3
regret, 130–32
resistant attachment, 72–73

safety, in therapeutic relationship, 103–5
Sandler, A. and J., 36
secure attachment, 72, 76
self: versus character structure, 9; states of, 88; types of, 88–89
self-determination, 147–48
self-representation, 11
separation, 71–75
sexual desire, 79–80
shame, 66–71; nature of, 68–69; psychotherapy and, 127
Shengold, L., 68
simplification, tendency toward, 55–57, 140
Smith, H. F., 139
soothing techniques, 5
Sophie (patient): and attribution error, 58–59; and defenses, 84–85; and forgiving, 142
soul murder, 68
South African Truth and Reconciliation Commission, 121
Spence, D., 107
subjectivity, psychotherapy and, 123–24
sympathy, 97
symptoms, and memory, 34–35

themes: central, 41; and interpretation, 108
therapeutic interventions, 95–119; content and context of, 95–97
therapy. *See* psychotherapy
transference, 112–15; and nonconscious phenomena, 26–27; relation to countertransference, 114–15
transformation, 112, 118–19
trauma: and adaptation, 52–54; and memory, 137; reconstruction and, 37
true self, 88–89
Truth and Reconciliation Commission, South Africa, 121

unconscious communication, 26, 30–31
unconscious phenomena, 26–33; psychotherapy and, 128
unforgivable actions, 141–42
upstairs-downstairs analogy, 26–33, 128

Winnicott, D., 125

About the Author

Dr. Robert E. Hooberman is a psychologist and psychoanalyst practicing in Ann Arbor, Michigan, where he treats adolescents, adults, and couples. In addition, he supervises other professionals and graduate students in the practice of psychotherapy and psychoanalysis. He is the author of three previous books, has written a number of articles on psychoanalysis and psychotherapy, and has presented numerous times locally and nationally. Dr. Hooberman is former president and former director of training for the Michigan Psychoanalytic Council. His scholarly interests revolve around the integration of psychodynamic theory and practice, on treating those who present special challenges to therapists, and on the evolving nature of the patient-therapist relationship.

www.ingramcontent.com/pod-product-compliance
Ingram Content Group UK Ltd.
Pitfield, Milton Keynes, MK11 3LW, UK
UKHW012041150926
475560UK00001B/127

9 780765 706676